SPACE

This edition published by Parragon in 2014
Parragon
Chartist House,
15-17 Trim Street,
Bath, BA1 1HA, UK
www.parragon.com

Copyright © Parragon Books Ltd 2001-2014

Written by: Anita Ganeri, John Malam, Clare Oliver and Adam Hibbert
Illustrated by: John Butler, Jim Eldridge, James Field, Andrew & Angela Harland, Colin Howard, Rob Jakeway, Mike Lacey, Sarah Lees, Gilly Marklew, Dud Moseley, Terry Riley, Sarah Smith, Stephen Sweet, Mike Taylor, Ross Watton (SGA) and Ian Thompso
Cartoonist: Peter Wilks (SGA)
Consultant: Steve Parker
This edition designed by Design Principals and Starry Dog Books.

All rights reserved. No part of this publication may be reproduced, stored in a retrieval system or transmitted, in any form or by any means, electronic, mechanical, photocopying, recording or otherwise, without the prior permission of the copyright holder.

ISBN 978-1-4723-0320-2

Printed in China

SPACE

PaRragon

Bath • New York • Singapore • Hong Kong • Cologne • Delhi
Melbourne • Amsterdam • Johannesburg • Auckland • Shenzhen

Contents

**CHAPTER ONE
OUR SOLAR SYSTEM**

10 What is the Solar System?

12 How hot is the Sun?

14 What does Mercury look like?

16 When is a star not a star?

18 What's special about our planet?

20 Why does the Moon change shape?

22 Does Mars have ice at its poles?

24 Which is the biggest planet?

26 Which world has the most volcanoes?

28 Are Saturn's rings solid?

30 Which planet was found by accident?

32 Which planet has pulling power?

34 Why is Pluto so cold?

36 Are there snowballs in space?

38 Quiz

CHAPTER TWO
SPACE EXPLORATION

42 Who made the first rockets?

44 Why do we need rockets?

46 Who was the first man in space?

48 Which astronauts went to sea?

50 Who first set foot on the Moon?

52 What was the first reusable spacecraft?

54 Why do astronauts wear space suits?

56 What's on the menu in space?

58 Which was the first space station?

60 Who needs a tool kit in space?

62 Has anyone ever been to Mars?

64 Which was the first satellite in space?

66 Which probe snapped a comet?

68 Might there be pirates in space?

70 Quiz

CHAPTER THREE
BEYOND OUR SOLAR SYSTEM

74 What is the Universe?

76 When did the Universe begin?

78 Will the Universe ever end?

80 What are star nurseries?

82 Which stars live together?

84 Which stars go out with a bang?

86 What is the Little Green Man?

88 What is a black hole?

90 What is a galaxy?

92 What shape is our galaxy?

94 Do galaxies stick together?

96 What is gravity?

98 Is time the same everywhere?

100 Is there anybody out there?

102 Quiz

CHAPTER FOUR
LOOKING AT THE NIGHT SKY

106 Who gazes at the stars?

108 Who built a tomb for the Sun god?

110 Who first wrote about the stars?

112 Who thought the Sun was as wide as a ruler?

114 Why do stars make patterns?

116 How did sailors know where they were going?

118 Who made the first telescope?

120 Who said that planets go round the Sun?

122 Where do astronomers put their telescopes?

124 How deep is space?

126 Who made the first radio telescope?

128 What's a gravity telescope?

130 Are there telescopes in space?

132 What's better than a powerful telescope?

134 Quiz

136 Answers to page 38 quiz

137 Answers to page 70 quiz

138 Answers to page 102 quiz

139 Answers to page 134 quiz

140 Glossary

142 Index

CHAPTER ONE

OUR SOLAR SYSTEM

❓ What is the Solar System?

Solar means 'of the Sun'. The Solar System is centred around the Sun, the shining ball in the sky. It includes the family of eight planets orbiting (travelling around) the Sun, as well as the moons of these planets and smaller objects, such as comets, asteroids and bits of space rock. The powerful pull of an invisible force called gravity from the Sun stops these bodies from flying off into deepest space.

Saturn
Distance from Sun
1,427 million km
Diameter
129,660 km

Jupiter
Distance from Sun
778 million km
Diameter
142,984 km

Mars
Distance from Sun
228 million km
Diameter
6,796 km

Venus
Distance from Sun
108 million km
Diameter
12,104 km

Mercury
Distance from Sun
58 million km
Diameter
4,878 km

Earth
Distance from Sun
150 million km
Diameter
12,756 km

Uranus
Distance from Sun
2,870 million km
Diameter
51,118 km

Neptune
Distance from Sun
4,497 million km
Diameter
49,532 km

Pluto
Distance from Sun
5,900 million km
Diameter
2,360 km

 Is it true?
All planets have one moon.

NO. Our planet Earth has one moon, called the Moon. But many of the planets have more than one. Our neighbour Mars, for instance, has two! Only the two planets closest to the Sun – Mercury and Venus – have no moons at all.

 Amazing! Saturn's not the only planet with rings. Saturn's rings are the easiest to see, but Jupiter, Neptune and Uranus have them, too. Saturn has seven main rings and then hundreds of thinner rings, called ringlets.

How hot is the Sun?

In deserts here on Earth, heat that has travelled 150 million km from the Sun can be hot enough to fry an egg. The Sun's surface is a super-hot 6,000°C, and its centre or core is even hotter.

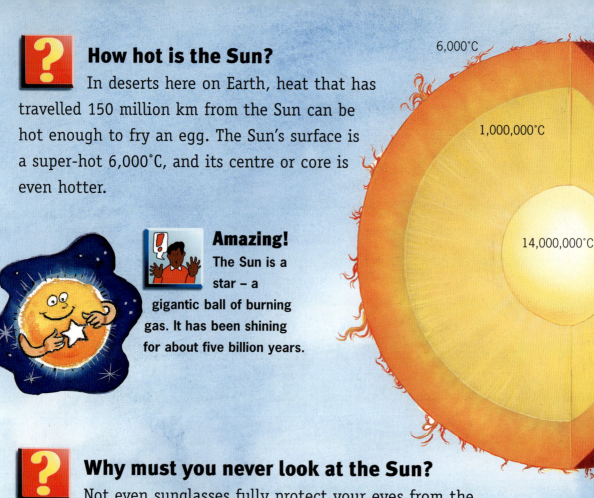

6,000°C

1,000,000°C

14,000,000°C

Amazing!
The Sun is a star – a gigantic ball of burning gas. It has been shining for about five billion years.

Why must you never look at the Sun?

Not even sunglasses fully protect your eyes from the Sun's dangerous ultraviolet (UV) rays. UV can burn your eyes and make you blind. If you want to see the Sun safely, ask an adult to show you how to project its image on to a sheet of paper.

Is it true?

The Sun has spots.

YES. The Sun is not the same colour all over. Some areas of its surface are darker. These spots are little pockets that are slightly cooler. Of course, sunspots are only 'little' compared to the Sun – some grow to be as large as Jupiter, the biggest planet in the Solar System!

WARNING!
Never look at the Sun, even if you're wearing sunglasses.

Total eclipse of the Sun

When does the Sun go out?

When there's a total eclipse. This happens when the Moon's path takes it between the Earth and the Sun, and the Moon casts a shadow across the surface of the Earth.

What does Mercury look like?

Planet Mercury looks very like our Moon. It's about the same size and it's covered in craters, where bits of space rock have crash-landed on its surface. The biggest crater is the Caloris Basin, which is about 1,300 km across. Mercury also has huge plains, rolling hills, deep gorges, chasms and cliffs.

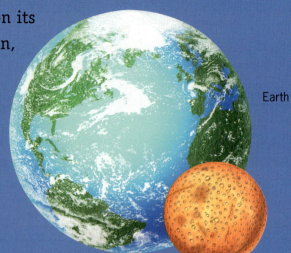

Earth

Mercury

The surface of Mercury is covered with craters

Is it true?
Mercury is the smallest planet.

YES. Now that Pluto is not considered to be a part of the Solar System, the planet Mercury, which is about a third the size of the Earth, is the smallest planet.

 **Is Mercury the hottest planet?**

Mercury is the planet closest to the Sun, but its neighbour, Venus, is even hotter, because it has clouds to keep in the heat.

The surface of Mercury is 350°C during the day and minus 170°C at night

 What is the weather like on Mercury?

Mercury doesn't have any weather, because it has no air and hardly any atmosphere. That means there are no clouds to shield the surface of the planet from the baking-hot Sun during the day, or to keep in the heat at night. There is no wind or rain on Mercury, either.

 Amazing! Mercury is the fastest planet. Mercury zooms around the Sun in just 88 days, at an incredible 173,000 kph. That makes it faster than any space rocket ever invented.

The planet Venus seen close to the Moon

When is a star not a star?

When it's a planet! Venus is sometimes called the 'evening star' because it's so bright it's one of the first points of light we see shining as it gets dark. Planets don't make their own light – they reflect the Sun's light.

 Is it true?
Venus is bigger than the Earth.

NO. Venus is a fraction smaller than the Earth, but not by much. Venus is about 12,104 km across, whereas Earth is about 650 km wider. Venus' mass is about four-fifths of Earth's.

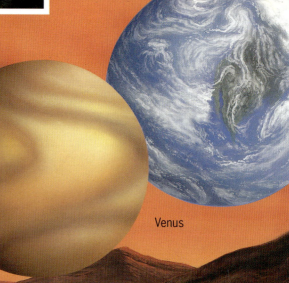

Earth

Venus

How can a day be longer than a year?

A day is the amount of time a planet takes to spin on its axis, and a year is the time it takes to travel around the Sun. Venus spins on its axis very slowly, but orbits the Sun more quickly than Earth. A day on Venus lasts 243 Earth-days, but a year is only 225 Earth-days.

Volcanic eruption on Venus

Amazing!
Venus is named after a goddess. Venus was the name of the Roman goddess of love and beauty – just right for the planet, which many people think is the most beautiful object in the sky.

What's special about our planet?

As far as we know, Earth is the only planet in the Solar System that has life. As well as warmth from the Sun, the other main ingredient for life is liquid water. Earth has plenty of water – in total, it covers about three-quarters of the planet's surface!

Earth seen from space

 Is it true?
There was life on Earth from the start.

NO. When Earth first formed it was extremely hot and there was no oxygen. Over millions of years, the planet cooled, oceans formed and oxygen was made. The first life on Earth appeared about 3 billion years ago.

What does Earth look like from space?

It looks beautiful – blue with swirling white clouds. Astronauts in space spend most of their free time gazing at it. They can even make out cities, when they are lit up at night with twinkling lights.

Amazing!
The Earth is magnetic. At the centre of the Earth is a core of a molten metal called iron, which makes our planet like a giant magnet. This is what pulls the needle on a compass towards the magnetic North Pole.

Why does our sky go dark at night?

Like all planets, the Earth is spinning as it orbits the Sun. When your part of the planet is facing away from the Sun, its light is blocked out. At the same time, it is daytime for people on the opposite side of the Earth.

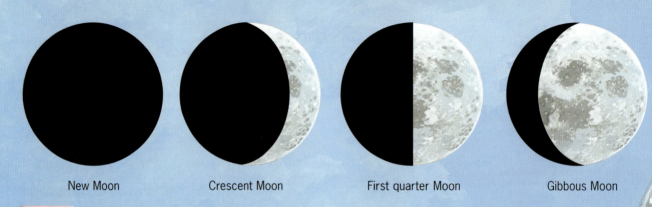

New Moon   Crescent Moon   First quarter Moon   Gibbous Moon

❓ Why does the Moon change shape?

It doesn't really – it's ball-shaped just like the Earth, but as the Moon travels around the Earth, you see different amounts of its sunlit half. It seems to change gradually from a crescent to a disc and back again.

❓ Why does the Moon have so many craters?

Because it has been pelted by so many space rocks and has no atmosphere to protect it. One of the biggest craters, called Bailly, is nearly 300 km across. You can make out some of the craters using a good pair of binoculars.

Meteorite hitting the Moon

Full Moon

 What is the dark side of the Moon?

It's the part of the Moon that we can never see from Earth. The Moon takes the same time to orbit the Earth as it does to spin once. This means the same side of the Moon always faces away from the Earth.

 Amazing! You can jump higher on the Moon. The Moon's gravity is much weaker than Earth's. This means you would only weigh about a sixth of your Earth-weight there – and you'd be able to jump six times higher!

 Is it true?
There are seas on the Moon.

YES AND NO. There are dark, rocky plains and craters called maria (Latin for 'seas'), but they don't contain water. The first astronauts to visit the Moon landed on the Sea of Tranquillity.

21

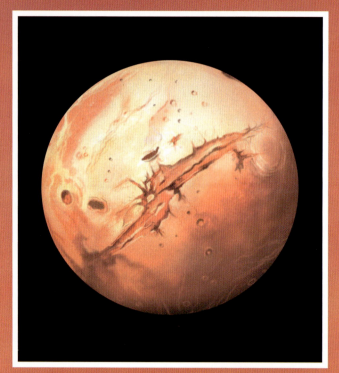
One of Mars's polar caps, at the bottom of the planet

 Does Mars have ice at its poles?
Yes. Its south pole is mostly 'dry ice', which is frozen carbon dioxide gas. At the north pole there may be frozen water, mixed with the frozen carbon dioxide. There may be frozen water underground on Mars, too.

Earth

Mars

Which is the red planet?
Mars was named after the Roman god of war, because of its blood-red colour. The planet looks rusty red because its surface is covered with iron-rich soil and rock. There are no seas on Mars and it is very cold.

The Martian surface, showing Olympus Mons

Is it true?
There is life on Mars.

NO. Or at least, there's no sure sign of any. But long ago, Mars had flowing rivers of water, so there could have been life once, and there may be fossils buried underground.

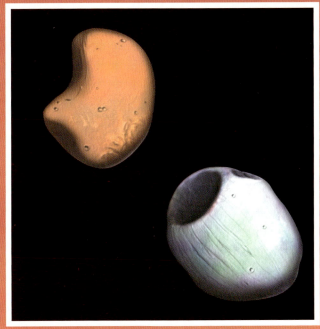

What are Mars's moons like?

Mars' two tiny moons, Deimos and Phobos, are not round like our Moon. They look more like baked potatoes! They might have been asteroids (space rocks) that Mars captured with its gravity.

Phobos
(about 15 km long)

Deimos
(about 27 km long)

Amazing! There's a record-breaking volcano on Mars. Olympus Mons is about 600 km across and towers over 25 km high. It's the Solar System's biggest volcano. Long ago it spurted out runny rivers of black lava.

? Which is the biggest planet?

Jupiter is so big that all the other planets in the Solar System could fit inside it! If it was any bigger it might become too hot in the middle, start to glow and turn into another Sun.

Is it true?
Jupiter's stripy.

YES. The planet looks like it's wearing a giant pair of pyjamas, because of its bands of cloud. They're made of frozen crystals of water, ammonia and other chemicals.

? What is Jupiter made of?

Jupiter is one of the planets known as the gas giants. About 90 per cent of it is made of gases called hydrogen and helium. At the centre of Jupiter is a small, rocky core, about as big as the Earth.

Core

Gases

Jupiter

Earth

Amazing! You could fit two Earths inside the Great Red Spot, which is about 40,000 km across.

Where is the storm that never stops?

Violent winds whip up storms all over the planet Jupiter, but the Great Red Spot is the largest. It has been raging away for over 300 years!

The Great Red Spot is a giant storm on Jupiter

Looking at Jupiter from Io

 Which world has the most volcanoes?

Jupiter's closest moon, Io, is orange and yellow, because of the sulphur from all its active volcanoes. If you could survive the intense heat, you'd realise that Io smells of rotten eggs!

Ganymede

 Which moon is bigger than a planet?

Jupiter's moon Ganymede is the largest moon in the Solar System. At 5,276 km across, it is bigger than Mercury! Another of Jupiter's moons, Callisto, is a similar size to Mercury.

Looking at Jupiter from Ganymede

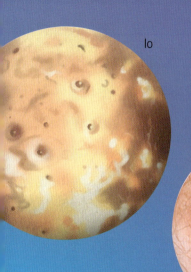
Io

Which moon might have life?
Jupiter's moon Europa is covered by a thick crust of ice. The ice looks smooth, like frozen water, but it also has lots of cracks. Scientists think there is a liquid ocean beneath the ice – and where there's water, there might be life!

Europa

 Amazing! Callisto is the most cratered world in the Solar System. Almost every bit of this moon is covered in craters. The biggest one is about 300 km across. It is called Valhalla, after the place where the Vikings thought brave warriors went when they died.

Callisto

 Is it true?
Jupiter only has four moons.

NO. Galileo discovered the four biggest – Callisto, Ganymede, Europa and Io – in 1610. Since then, astronomers have discovered many smaller moons as well, making a total of 50 moons so far.

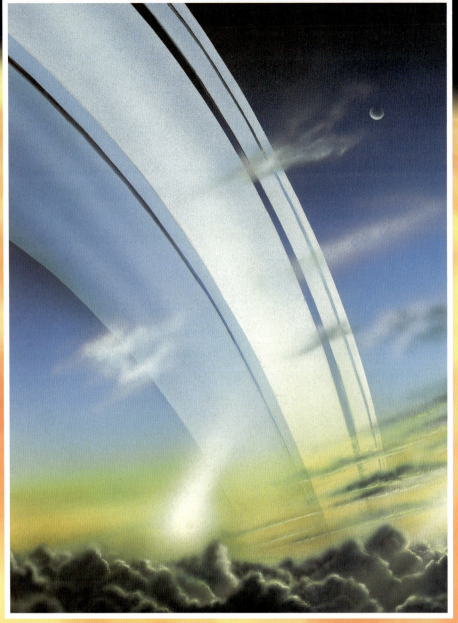

Saturn's rings viewed from its upper atmosphere

 Amazing! You could fit about 740 Earths into Saturn. It is the Solar System's second largest planet, after Jupiter. Its rings are 270,000 km across – about twice the width of the planet.

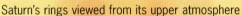 **Are Saturn's rings solid?**
No – they look solid, but they are made up of millions of chunks of ice and rock. The smallest chunks are about the size of a golf ball, while the biggest are about a kilometre wide.

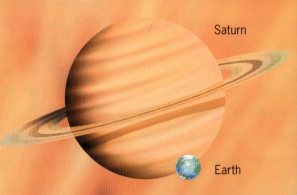
Saturn

Earth

Saturn viewed from above Titan

 Do Saturn's rings have names?

Not really, but scientists have given each ring a letter so that they know which one they are talking about. There are seven main rings, of which the three brightest are A, B and C.

 How many moons does Saturn have?

Saturn has about 62 moons, but there may be more. The biggest is Titan – the second largest moon in the Solar System. Titan is covered by clouds, so we can't see its surface.

 Is it true?
Saturn is light enough to float.

YES. Saturn is made up of liquid and gas, with a small rocky centre. It is so light that, if there was an ocean big enough, the planet would float on it like a boat!

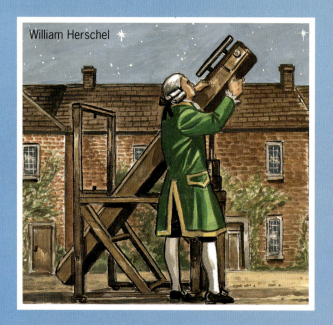
William Herschel

 Which planet was found by accident?

Uranus was discovered in 1781. The man who found it, William Herschel, was not expecting to find a planet at all. He thought he was pointing his homemade telescope at a distant star.

 How many moons does Uranus have?

Uranus has about 27 moons – but there could be more to discover. They are all named after characters from English literature. The main ones are Oberon, Titania, Umbriel, Ariel and Miranda. Ophelia and Cordelia are the closest.

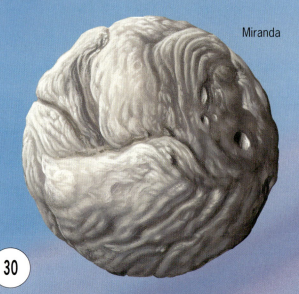
Miranda

 Amazing! The poles on Uranus are warmer than the equator. Because Uranus is tilted on its side, the poles are the warmest places on the planet. Summer at the south pole lasts 42 years!

Approaching Uranus through its rings

Uranus
Earth

Why is Uranus blue?

The bluish-green is the colour of methane, a stinky gas that makes up part of Uranus' atmosphere. The other gases in the air there are hydrogen and helium – the gas we use to fill party balloons.

Is it true?
Uranus was nearly called George.

YES. When Herschel discovered the new planet, he wanted to name it after the English king at the time, George III. In the end, it was called Uranus, after the Greek god of the sky.

Which planet has pulling power?

Astronomers knew Neptune must be there before they saw it! They could tell something big was pulling Uranus and they were able to predict exactly where Neptune was – almost 4.5 billion kilometres away from the Sun.

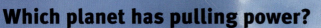

Storm on Neptune

What's the weather like on Neptune?

Very, very windy! Winds rip across the planet all the time, much faster than any winds on Earth. There are also lots of storms on Neptune, which show up as dark spots. This means Neptune's appearance is constantly changing.

 Amazing! Triton is one of the coldest places ever recorded! The temperature on the ice-covered moon is minus 236°C. That's just 37°C away from being the lowest possible temperature in the entire Universe!

Neptune's windy surface

Is it true?
Triton is Neptune's only moon.

NO. Neptune has 13 other moons, but Triton and Nereid are the main ones. Triton is the biggest. It is 2,706 km across – about four-fifths the size of our moon.

? Where would you find pink snow?
When the gas nitrogen freezes, it looks like pink snow! There is frozen nitrogen at Neptune's north and south poles, and at the poles of its largest moon, Triton. So far from the Sun, Neptune and its moons are bitterly cold places.

Neptune seen from Triton.

Pluto's icy surface is minus 220°C

❓ Why is Pluto so cold?

Pluto is very far from the Sun—almost 5,900 million km away. Inside, it is made up of ice and rock, and it has a thick layer of ice over the top.

 Is it true?
Pluto was named after a cartoon dog.

NO. Pluto was the name of the Greek god of the underworld. Also, the first two letters of Pluto, 'P' and 'L', are the initials of Percival Lowell, who initiated the research efforts that later led to the discovery of Pluto.

❓ Who found Pluto's moon?

An American called Jim Christy discovered Pluto's moon in 1978. He called it Charon, which was his wife's name and also the name of the man who ferried people to the underworld in Ancient Greek mythology.

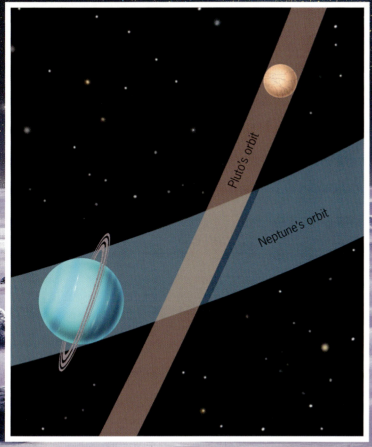

 Is Pluto always far from the Sun?

Pluto is so far away from the Sun that it takes 248 years just to orbit it once! But Pluto's orbit is a funny shape. For 20 years of its orbit, Pluto dips in closer to the Sun than Neptune.

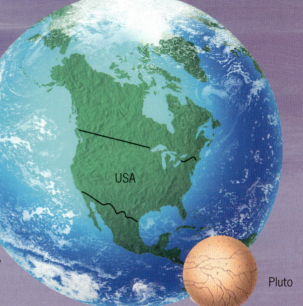

Pluto

 Amazing! Pluto is smaller than a country. At 2,360 km across, it is smaller than the United States or Russia!

Are there snowballs in space?

Yes – comets are balls of ice and rock. They go whizzing through the Solar System leaving behind a glowing tail of gas. As a comet gets closer to the Sun, it gets hotter and its tail becomes longer. Some comets even grow a second tail. In the past, the arrival of a comet was thought to be a magical event.

Amazing! We can tell when comets will come back. Some comets follow a regular course, so we know exactly when we'll next see them. Halley's Comet will next fly past the Earth in 2061.

Are there any minor planets?

There are lots of minor planets, known as asteroids, in our Solar System. More than 3,500 of these lumps of space rock are orbiting the Sun.

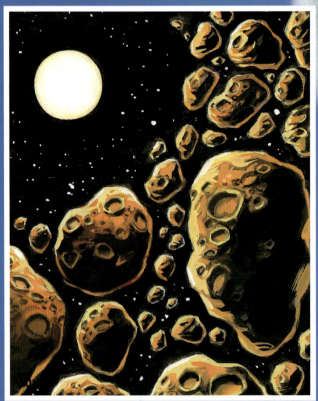

Asteroids orbiting the Sun

Is it true?
Asteroids weigh the same as the Earth.

NO. Even if all of the asteroids in the Solar System were lumped together, the Earth would still weigh more than a thousand times as much.

Comet with its glowing tail

What is a shooting star?

A shooting star, or meteor, happens when a tiny space rock, called a meteoroid, enters Earth's atmosphere and burns up. We see it as a streak of light across the sky. Meteor showers happen when our planet passes through a group of meteoroids.

Shooting stars

QUICK QUIZ

1. What does 'solar' mean?
2. How many planets orbit the Sun?
3. How many moons does Mars have?
4. Are sunspots hotter or cooler than the rest of the Sun?
5. Which is the hottest planet?

6. Does Mercury travel faster than a space rocket?
7. Which planet is sometimes called the 'evening star'?
8. Who is Venus named after?
9. How much of the Earth's surface is covered in water?
10. Which molten metal forms the Earth's core?

11. What was the name of the sea where the first astronauts to visit the Moon landed?

12. What makes the craters on the Moon's surface?

13. What is the name of the biggest volcano in the Solar System, found on Mars?

14. What is Jupiter's Great Red Spot?

15. What does Io smell of?

16. How many moons does Jupiter have?

17. Is Saturn bigger or smaller than Earth?

18. What is the name of Saturn's biggest moon?

19. What lasts for 42 years on Uranus?

20. What colour is Uranus?

21. What is Triton covered in?

22. Which is the smallest planet in the Solar System?

23. Which is bigger, Russia or Pluto?

24. What is a comet made of?

25. What is another name for a shooting star?

Answers on page 136.

CHAPTER TWO

SPACE EXPLORATION

Who made the first rockets?

The Chinese made the first 'rockets' about 1,000 years ago, but they were more like fireworks than today's space rockets. They were flaming arrows that were fired from a basket using gunpowder.

Chinese 'rocket'

 Amazing! You don't need to be a rocket scientist to build rockets. Lots of people make mini rockets as a hobby. There is even a yearly contest, when people show off their latest creations!

Is it true?
Thrust SSC is a rocket-powered car.

NO. Thrust SSC, one of the fastest cars, has two jet engines. A jet engine could not power a space mission, because it needs air and there's no air in space.

❓ When did the first liquid-fuel rocket fly?

In 1926, American Robert Goddard launched a 3.5 metre-long rocket. It flew about as high as a two-storey house, nowhere near outer space, and landed 56 metres away. The flight lasted just two-and-a-half seconds.

Goddard's rocket

❓ Who built a rocket for war?

Wernher von Braun invented the V2, a rocket missile used by the Germans in World War II. After the war, von Braun moved to the United States, to help with the new American space programme.

von Braun and V2 missile

Why do we need rockets?

Rockets are important for space travel. They are the only machines powerful enough to launch things into space, such as satellites, probes and people. All the parts needed to build space stations have been carried up by rockets.

Ariane releasing a satellite

Amazing! The European Ariane rocket could carry a fully grown elephant. Ariane's biggest payload (cargo) so far is a satellite which weighed 4.6 tonnes.

How fast can a rocket go?

To escape from Earth's gravity, a rocket has to reach 40,000 kph – almost 20 times faster than supersonic Concorde. Once it is out in space, the rocket drops down to around 29,000 kph to stay in orbit.

Saturn 5 rocket

Rocket stages falling away

Is it true?
Saturn 5 rockets were as tall as a 30-storey building.

YES. At 111 metres high, the Saturn 5 was the tallest rocket ever made. Most of the rocket fell away once it had done its job.

Why do rockets fall to pieces?

Rockets are made in stages, or pieces. Usually, there are three stages, made up of the fuel and rocket engines. Each stage drops off when its job is done. It takes a huge amount of power to push a heavy rocket into space.

Amazing! The first living creature in space was a Russian dog, called Laika. She made a seven-day journey in the space capsule Sputnik 2 in November 1957.

Voskhod spacecraft

Yuri Gagarin and Vostok 1

Who was the first man in space?

A young Russian pilot called Yuri Gagarin was the first person in space. He orbited the Earth in a small capsule called Vostok 1 on 12 April 1961. His journey lasted less than two hours.

Who was the first woman in space?

The first woman in space was Russian, too. Valentina Tereshkova made a three-day space journey in Vostok 6 in 1963. The first American woman in space was Sally Ride, in 1983.

Valentina Tereshkova

Alexei Leonov making the first spacewalk

Who took the first spacewalk?

The cosmonaut (Russian astronaut) Alexei Leonov took a ten-minute spacewalk on 18 March 1965. To make sure he didn't float off, Leonov tied himself to his capsule.

Is it true?
A chimp could survive a space flight.

YES. Ham was the first to try out the Mercury capsule, in 1961. Despite travelling at 8,045 kph, the chimpanzee survived the 16-minute flight.

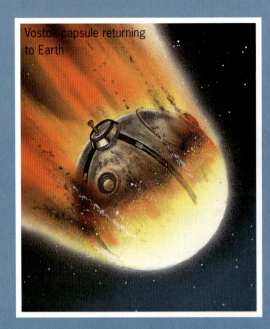
Vostok capsule returning to Earth

 Which astronauts went to sea?

American astronauts returning to Earth landed in the sea and were picked up by helicopter. Their capsules had huge parachutes to slow down their fall and rubber rings, so that they would float.

Apollo capsule splashing down

Amazing! Capsules got extremely hot. When a capsule re-entered Earth's atmosphere, its surface heated it up to 3,000°C – twice the temperature needed to melt iron. But they didn't melt, because they were protected by a special heat shield.

Who came down to Earth with a bang?

Russian capsules landed on hard ground. The cosmonauts bailed out and parachuted down the last few kilometres, but even so, many broke a few bones. They usually had to spend months in hospital recovering from the landing.

Cosmonaut ejecting

Who knew where astronauts landed?

Machinery on board a capsule was radio-linked to Mission Control (the people on the ground in charge of a space mission). This meant people knew exactly where to find the astronauts – usually!

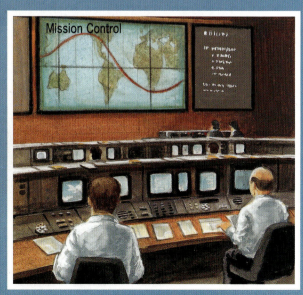

 Is it true?
Voskhod 2 got lost.

YES. Voskhod 2 was the capsule carrying Alexei Leonov, the first spacewalker. The auto-pilot machinery went wrong and the capsule ended up 1,000 km off-course, in a snowy forest!

Neil Armstrong

❓ Who first set foot on the Moon?

The very first person to step on to the Moon was the American Neil Armstrong, in 1969. He had flown there in Apollo 11 with Buzz Aldrin, who followed him on to the Moon's surface, and Michael Collins.

Apollo 13

 Amazing! There should have been seven manned missions to the Moon. Two days into Apollo 13's journey to the Moon, its oxygen tanks exploded. It took a nail-biting four days to bring its crew safely back to Earth.

How many Moon missions were there?

There were six manned Apollo landings on the Moon, and about 80 unmanned ones too. Apollo 17 landed the last astronauts on the Moon in 1972.

Is it true?
There are footsteps on the Moon.

YES. There is no atmosphere on the Moon, which means there is no wind either. Tyre tracks and footprints in the dusty surface will be there for hundreds of years.

❓ Who first drove on the Moon?
In 1971, Apollo 15 carried a Lunar Rover. David Scott and James Irwin drove the battery-powered buggy over the Moon's cratered surface, collecting samples of Moon rock.

Lunar Rover

Is it true?
There was only room for five astronauts aboard the shuttle.

NO. The space shuttle was designed to carry eight astronauts, but it could carry ten at a pinch!

The shuttle was launched using two solid rocket boosters and three main rocket engines

Rocket boosters fall away

Lift off

What was the first reusable spacecraft?

The space shuttle was the first spacecraft designed to be used more than once. Not every part was reusable, because it needed new rocket boosters for each flight. The shuttles made over 100 missions into space. The first was Columbia, which blasted off in 1981. It orbited the Earth at about 27,840 kph – about ten times faster than a speeding bullet.

How many space shuttles were there?

Five space shuttles were built. The shuttle Challenger exploded shortly after lift-off in 1986 and the shuttle Columbia disintegrated re-entering the Earth's atmosphere in 2003. Shuttles were used for launching and repairing satellites, and space research.

Challenger explosion

Amazing! The Russian space shuttle, called Buran, only flew once, in 1988. Buran was carried into space by a rocket. Unlike the American shuttle, it was unmanned.

How did the shuttle land?

At the end of its mission, the shuttle dropped its speed to break orbit – on the opposite side of the world to the place it wanted to land. Then it turned off its engines and glided like a bird, landing on a runway about an hour later.

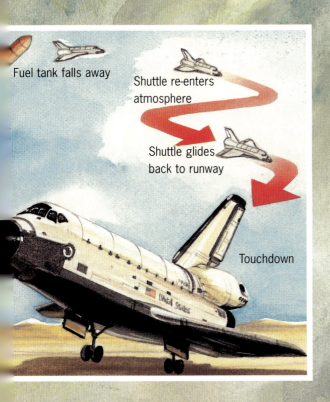
Fuel tank falls away
Shuttle re-enters atmosphere
Shuttle glides back to runway
Touchdown

❓ Why do astronauts wear space suits?

Space suits act like a suit of armour. They stop an astronaut's blood boiling in space and reflect the Sun's dangerous rays. They have a built-in backpack, containing an oxygen supply, battery and cooling system.

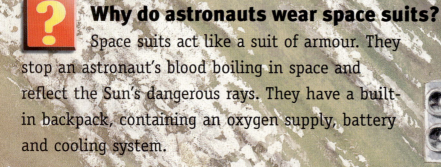

Cutaway of helmet shows communications headset

Cutaway of space suit shows water-cooling tubes stitched into undergarment

Amazing! Astronauts are water-cooled! A system of tubes sewn into the space suit carries cool liquid around to keep the astronaut's temperature normal.

 Is it true?
Cosmonauts took off in their underwear.

YES. In the early days of Russian space travel, space suits were worn only for spacewalks. Some cosmonauts just wore their underwear at take-off time!

Cosmonaut in space capsule

? Do astronauts wear space suits all the time?

No. They wear them for spacewalks and during take-off, landing or when they dock with another craft. The rest of the time, astronauts wear shorts and a tee shirt.

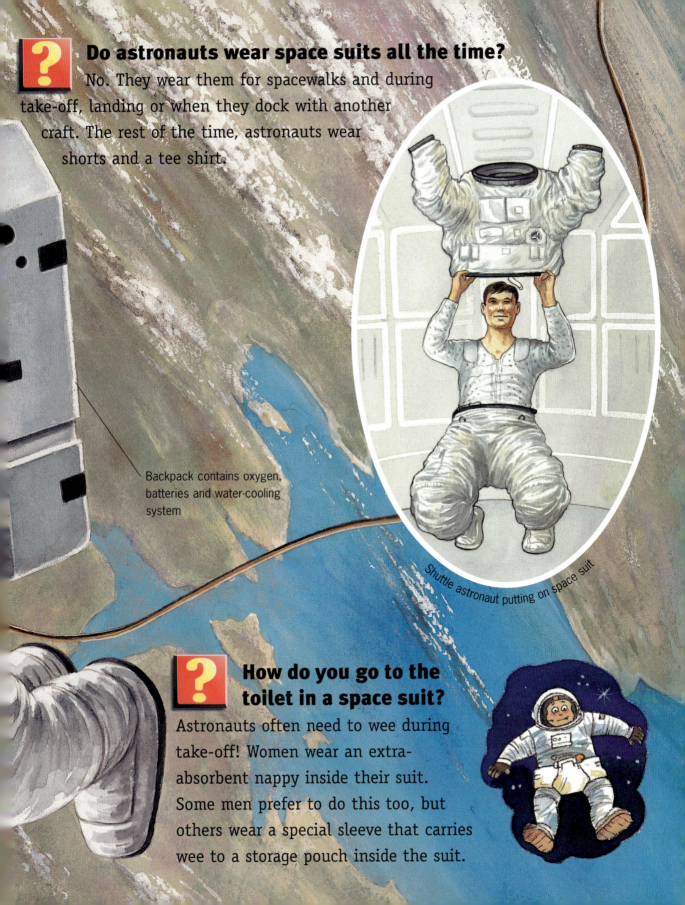

Backpack contains oxygen, batteries and water-cooling system

Shuttle astronaut putting on space suit

? How do you go to the toilet in a space suit?

Astronauts often need to wee during take-off! Women wear an extra-absorbent nappy inside their suit. Some men prefer to do this too, but others wear a special sleeve that carries wee to a storage pouch inside the suit.

What's on the menu in space?

Astronauts either add water to waterless food, or they eat ready meals, such as stew or pasta. Canned fruit, puddings, biscuits, sweets and gum are all on the menu, too.

Space shuttle galley

Is it true?
Astronauts eat freeze-dried ice cream.

NO. The 'astronaut ice cream' sold in the shops isn't really eaten in space. But on the Mir space station, American astronauts took out an ice cream feast to share with the Russian cosmonauts!

Why doesn't the food float away?

Everything floats about in space, so meals are eaten from trays stuck to astronauts' clothes. Drinks come in a cup with a lid and are sucked up through a straw.

Eating in space

 Amazing! Some astronauts get space sickness! Floating makes many astronauts throw up and if they're not careful the sick flies everywhere! Luckily, the sickness wears off after a day or two.

Skylab shower

How do astronauts wash?

The Skylab space station had a shower fitted with a vacuum cleaner to suck off the water, but there was no room for a shower on the shuttle. Astronauts used wet wipes and cleaned their hair with rinseless shampoo.

Amazing! There were spiders in space. Arabella and Anita had a special mission on Skylab. Scientists wanted to see if space affected how spiders spin webs.

Soyuz spacecraft docked with Salyut 1 space station

Which was the first space station?

The first manned space station was Salyut 1, launched in 1971, which had room for three crew. It was meant to go into permanent orbit around the Earth, but its orbit was a bit too low.

What happens in a space station?

Astronauts live in space stations for weeks or even months. They do experiments and find out more about space. They also do lots of exercise, to stay fit and healthy.

Exercise in space

Is it true?
Your bones get weaker in space.

YES. This isn't serious on short missions, but no one knows what would happen if you spent years in space.

Which is the biggest space station?

The International Space Station (ISS) is the biggest ever space station. The first module was launched in 1998 and the space station's parts are being built by 16 countries.

International Space Station

❓ Who needs a tool kit in space?

Astronauts need tools to build the ISS and repair satellites. In 1993, a space shuttle crew repaired the Hubble Space Telescope.

Working in space

MMU in action

❓ What's an MMU?

MMU stands for Manned Manoeuvring Unit. It's like an armchair that carries an astronaut around in space, when he or she is outside the spacecraft. It uses 24 little gas jets to move backwards or forwards, up or down.

Is it true?
The space shuttle had an arm.

YES. It had a robot arm with a hand that could grip at the end. It could be controlled by astronauts inside or outside the shuttle. The robot arm was useful for picking up objects in space.

 Amazing! Astronauts train underwater. Working underwater gives astronauts an idea of how it will feel to float in space. Water makes an astronaut's body move in the opposite direction when they try to pull or push something, just as it would in space.

Astronaut using headset radio

 ## How do astronauts talk to each other?

Space is an airless vacuum that won't carry sound. Even if they were yelling, astronauts outside their craft wouldn't be able to hear each other, so they stay in touch by radio.

Has anyone ever been to Mars?

No, not yet, anyway! The distance from Earth to Mars varies from 56 million km to 400 million km. Even at its closest, Mars would be a six-month journey away.

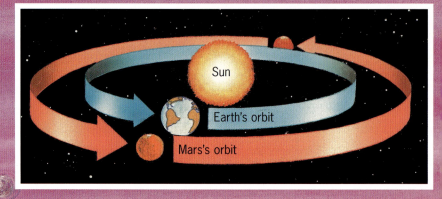

Pathfinder landing

Is it true?
Vikings landed on Mars.

YES. In 1976, two space probes called Vikings 1 and 2 landed there. During their mission, they collected samples and took over 3,000 photos.

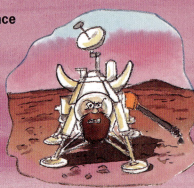

What used balloons to land on Mars?

The Mars Pathfinder probe entered the Martian atmosphere on 4 July 1997. It used a parachute and rockets to slow down and then a bundle of balloons inflated around it so that it could bounce safely down on to the surface.

 Amazing! Pathfinder landed in a river! Although there is no liquid water on Mars now, the rocky plain where Pathfinder touched down showed signs that water had flowed there once.

Pathfinder

 Which robot first explored Mars?

Pathfinder carried a robot car called Sojourner, which was radio-controlled from Earth. It had a camera and devices for studying the soil and rock.

Which was the first satellite in space?
Sputnik 1 was the first satellite to orbit the Earth. It was launched by the Russians in October 1957 and took 90 minutes to circle the planet.

Is it true?
A person could have fitted in Sputnik 1.

NO. The satellite was less than 60 cm across – smaller than most beach balls! Sputnik was just a radio transmitter really, but it was very important for space exploration.

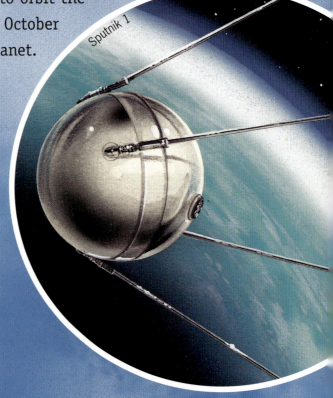

Sputnik 1

 ## Can you see any satellites from Earth?
Yes. You can see satellites moving across the sky when the Sun is shining on them but it is dark on Earth. The best times to spot satellites are the two hours after sunset and the two hours before sunrise.

Amazing! Satellites are powered by the Sun. Rocket power takes satellites up into orbit, but once they're there, they use special solar panels to collect energy from the Sun. This is turned into electricity to power the satellites' batteries.

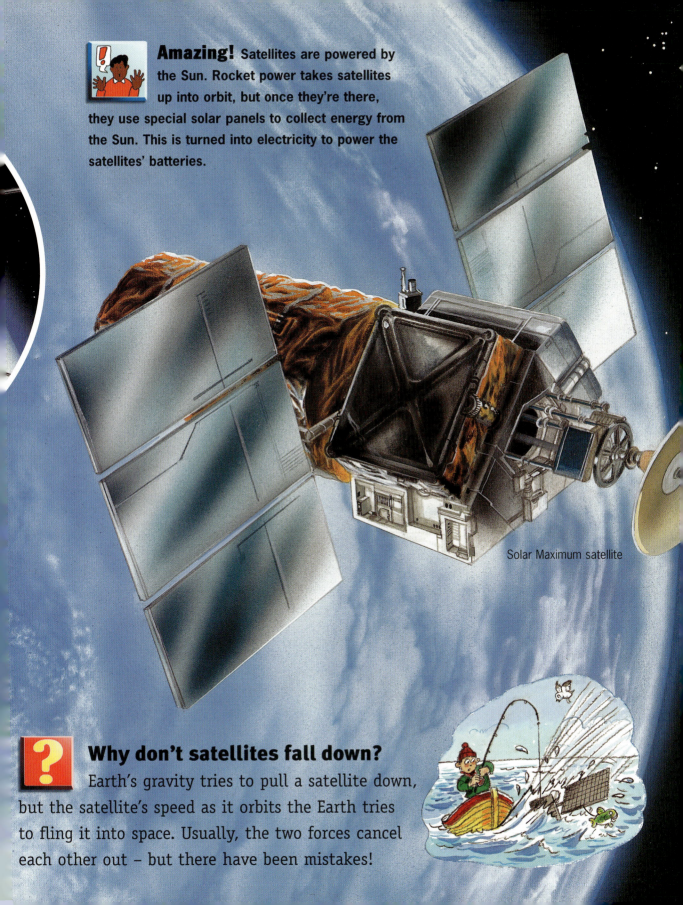

Solar Maximum satellite

Why don't satellites fall down?
Earth's gravity tries to pull a satellite down, but the satellite's speed as it orbits the Earth tries to fling it into space. Usually, the two forces cancel each other out – but there have been mistakes!

Which probe snapped a comet?

The Giotto space probe visited Halley's Comet in 1986 and took brilliant photos of the comet's rocky core. Even though Giotto kept a safe distance of about 600 km, its special protective shields got covered in icy dust.

Halley's Comet

Giotto

 Amazing! A probe carries a message for aliens. The Pioneer 10 probe was fitted with a plaque, just in case it's ever found by aliens. It shows a man and woman, and a map to show where Earth is in the Universe.

Pioneer 10's plaque

Is it true?
A probe was made out of junk.

YES. Magellan, sent to visit Venus in 1989, was made up of spare parts from other missions.

Which spacecraft flew the furthest?

Voyager 2, launched in 1977, has flown past Jupiter, Saturn, Uranus and Neptune. Now it is beyond our Solar System, heading into interstellar space.

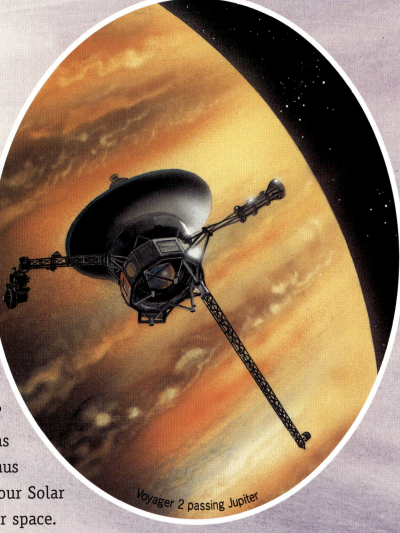

Voyager 2 passing Jupiter

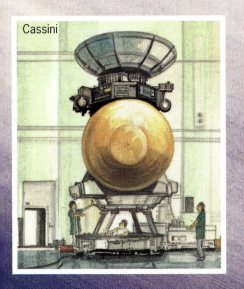

Cassini

Which probe was as big as a bus?

The bus-sized Cassini space probe had another probe, called Huygens, on board. It reached Saturn in 2004. Cassini beams data back to Earth about Saturn's rings, moons and the planet itself.

Moon Base of the future

 Is it true?
We could never breathe on Mars.

NO. We couldn't breathe in the atmosphere there as it is, but we could build airtight cities and grow plants there that would make oxygen for us.

? Might there be pirates in space?
If we ever set up space mining stations, spacecraft would zoom about the Solar System with very valuable cargoes. Space pirates might try to board cargo-carrying craft to rob them!

Will we ever live on the Moon?

There might be a Moon Base, one day. The Moon is only three days away and its low gravity makes it easy to land spacecraft there. It would be a good place for telescopes, because there is no atmosphere to distort the pictures.

Amazing! People are planning a space hotel. Holidays in space are not far off. There are plans for a doughnut-shaped space hotel, using old shuttle fuel tanks as rooms!

Will we ever live on other planets?

It will take a lot more probe missions before we could consider building bases on other planets. But if travel to other stars ever became possible, the outer planets could act as useful 'petrol stations'.

Space tanker near Saturn

QUICK QUIZ

1. Who made the first rockets?
2. What was a V2?
3. A rocket has to reach 40,000 kph to escape from what?
4. What was Laika famous for?
5. Who was the first person in space?

6. Astronauts and cosmonauts return to Earth in a what?
7. What protects an astronaut's capsule from burning up on re-entry to Earth's atmosphere?
8. Who first set foot on the Moon?
9. What exploded on Apollo 13?
10. What kind of vehicle did Apollo 15 carry to the Moon?

11. What was the name of the first space shuttle?
12. Did the Russians have a space shuttle?
13. What keeps an astronaut's space suit cool?
14. What did the first cosmonauts wear for take-off?
15. What do astronauts use to drink from?

16. On Skylab, what happened to the water in the shower?
17. Why were spiders sent into space?
18. What does ISS stand for?
19. What does MMU stand for?
20. What was the space shuttle's arm used for?

21. What did the Vikings do on Mars?

22. What was the name of the radio-controlled car that studied soil and rock samples on Mars?

23. Which was the first satellite in space?

24. What powers satellites?

25. Which comet was photographed by the Giotto space probe?

Answers on page 137.

CHAPTER THREE

BEYOND OUR SOLAR SYSTEM

What is the Universe?

Every person, planet, star and galaxy is part of the Universe – and even every empty space! The Universe is the biggest thing we have a word for.

Amazing! The Universe is too big to measure in kilometres. Even if you could travel at the speed of light, it would take at least 15 billion years to cross it – as far as we know!

What's outside the Universe?

It's impossible to say. Scientists are still trying to guess, by using clues left behind from the birth of our Universe. They are pretty sure there would be no time, distance or things there.

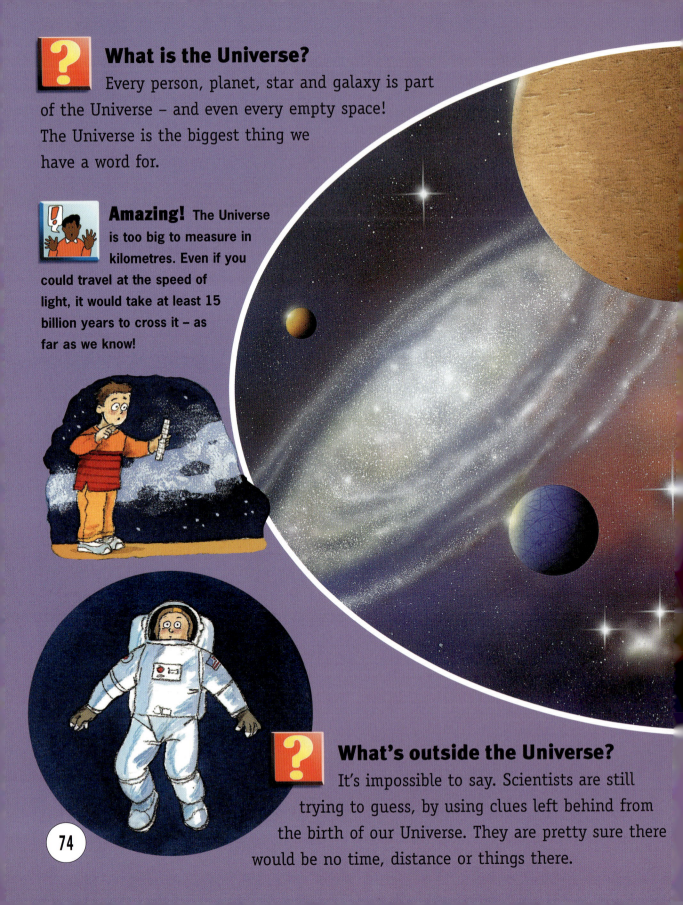

Where are we in the Universe?

People once thought Earth was at the centre of the Universe. Now we know Earth is one of many planets moving through space. It's hard to tell where we are because we can't see the Universe's edges.

Voyager space probe looking at our galaxy in the distant future

Our Solar System

Local stars

Our galaxy

Local group of galaxies

Local super group of galaxies

The Universe

Is it true?

There are more stars than people.

YES. As a rough guess, scientists think that there are about 1.8 million million stars for every human being alive in the world today.

The Universe expands from the Big Bang

When did the Universe begin?

Scientists have argued about this for centuries. At the moment, most people agree that the Universe began between 12 and 15 billion years ago. It all started with a mind-boggling explosion called the Big Bang.

 Amazing! The Big Bang was super-hot! Scientists don't even bother writing out all the zeros in its temperature. They write $10^{27}°C$, meaning 10 with 27 zeros after it!

What was the Big Bang?

It was a huge explosion, that created all the mass and energy in our Universe in less than a second! The effects of the blast are so strong that the Universe is still expanding.

Is it true?
You could see the Big Bang through a telescope.

NEARLY. Our telescopes aren't powerful enough yet – but we can already see light from the other side of the Universe that began its journey just after the Big Bang!

What if the Big Bang happened again?

It couldn't happen again in our Universe, but some people think it may be happening millions of times, making millions of different universes. Only a few would last as long as ours – most would pop like soap bubbles.

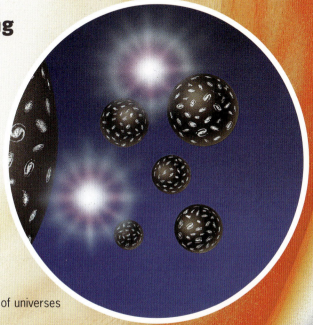

There might be millions of universes

❓ Will the Universe ever end?

Some cosmologists (people who study the Universe) believe that the Universe will eventually stop expanding outwards. They think it will shrink back to nothing in an event called the Big Crunch!

Is it true?
The Universe might just fizzle out.

YES. If the Universe keeps spreading out forever, it will get quite boring. After the stars have burnt out, there'll just be lumps of rock and dust floating around doing nothing!

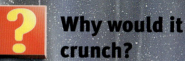 **Why would it crunch?**

The Universe is still blowing up, but there are lots of heavy things in it. Just like a toy balloon, which has run out of puff, gravity might pull the Universe back to where, and how, it started.

The Universe shrinks back to the Big Crunch

 Amazing! The Universe might go on forever! Some cosmologists think that the Universe will never stop expanding. They don't think gravity will ever be able to stop it, so it will just get bigger and bigger.

Will I see the Big Crunch?

Not unless you live forever! Even if the Universe does stop expanding, it will take about another 15 billion years to collapse in on itself in a Big Crunch.

What are star nurseries?

New stars are born in star nurseries – huge clouds of gas and dust known as nebulae (or nebula if you're just talking about one). Nebulae are some of the most beautiful sights that powerful telescopes have ever revealed.

Stars are born in gaseous clouds called nebulae

Amazing! A star can be born in a horse's head! The Horsehead Nebula is a glowing cloud of gas in another galaxy. It has a lump shaped like a horse's head, where stars are being born.

How are stars born?

The gases in a nebula gradually gather together into spinning balls. They spin more and more quickly, until they get amazingly hot and a big blast, called a nuclear reaction, begins. When this happens, a baby star begins to glow.

What are stars made of?

Stars are mostly made of two gases, hydrogen and helium. Helium is the gas used to fill party balloons. There are lots of layers inside a star, with gases moving around in each one.

 Is it true?
You are made of stardust.

YES. Everything in space, including you, is made out of elements, such as carbon and silicon. All of these were cooked up in stars, which formed from the first matter in the Universe.

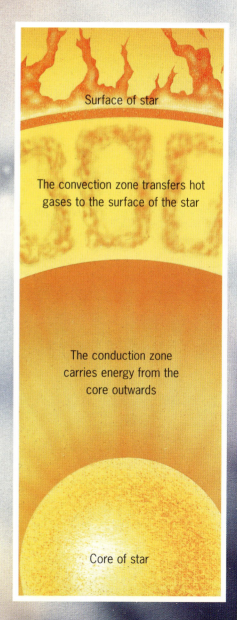

Surface of star

The convection zone transfers hot gases to the surface of the star

The conduction zone carries energy from the core outwards

Core of star

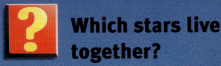

Which stars live together?

Our star, the Sun, is all alone, but some stars, called binary stars, are in pairs. They seem to spin around each other. Very close pairs do one turn of this 'dance' in just hours!

Binary stars viewed from a planet in deepest space

Our Sun is a medium-sized star

How long do stars shine for?

It depends. Very hot, bright stars burn up all their energy in a few million years. A star like our Sun, which is only medium-hot, can shine for billions of years.

What is a white giant?

White giants are really huge, hot stars that appear to be white. They can be 20 times bigger than our Sun. Rigel is a white giant shining about 60,000 times more brightly than our Sun.

Our Sun compared to a white giant

Amazing! Small stars are called dwarfs! Astronomers know that stars come in lots of different sizes. To make it easier to describe the sizes, they call big stars giants and little ones dwarfs.

Is it true?
Most stars are yellow.

NO. Stars hotter than our Sun often shine a bright pale blue, while other stars can sometimes appear red or white. Only a few are yellow.

Which stars go out with a bang?

Really massive stars, at least eight times bigger than our Sun, die in an explosion called a supernova. For a few days supernovas shine so strongly that, here on Earth, we can see them during the day.

Amazing! Supernovas are a very rare sight. Only a few supernovas have been seen in our galaxy in the last 1,000 years. One visible to the naked eye was seen in 1987, in a nearby galaxy called the Large Magellanic Cloud.

What is a white dwarf?

A white dwarf is a dying star. Its gas has burnt off and a planet-sized, white-hot and incredibly dense core is all that is left. Over billions of years, this fades and dies. Sirius B, or the 'Pup', is a white dwarf.

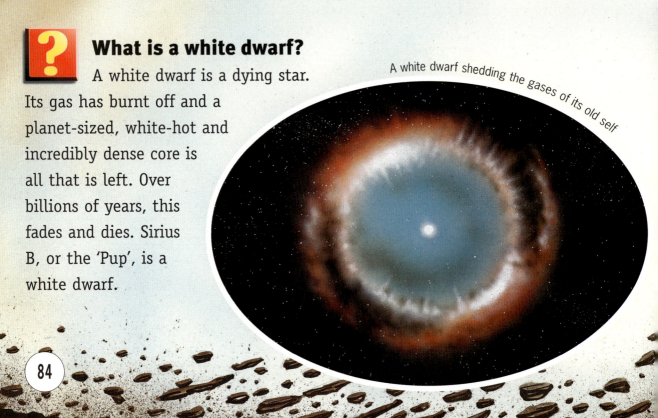

A white dwarf shedding the gases of its old self

What is a red giant?

A red giant is an old star that has swollen up. Depending how big it gets, it might blow up or fade out. Astronomers think that our Sun will grow into a red giant in about five billion years' time. Betelgeuse is a red giant and is 1000 times bigger than our Sun.

Our Sun compared to an enormous red giant

A red giant swallows up a planet

Is it true?
Dead stars are called black dwarfs.

YES. Once a white dwarf has cooled and stopped shining, it becomes a dead, black dwarf.

What is the Little Green Man?

LGM stands for 'Little Green Man'. LGM1 is a light deep in space that flashes 30 times a second. It is a pulsar – a tiny, dense neutron star (the remains of a supernova) that flashes out light and radio signals as it spins.

A pulsar flashing out light and radio signals, near a red giant

Is it true?
Scientists thought pulsar signals were messages from aliens.

YES. The astronomers in Cambridge, England, who discovered LGM1 wondered at first if they'd come across an alien distress beacon or some other kind of coded message!

AMAZING! Neutron stars are super-heavy! They can be just 20 km across, but weigh 50 times more than planet Earth!

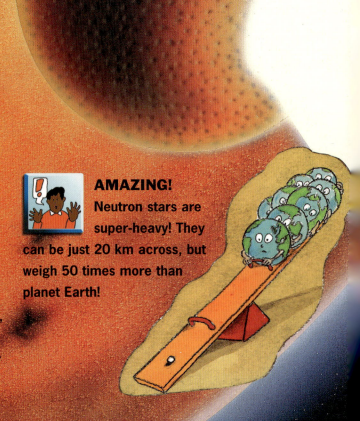

Radio telescopes

 How many pulsars are there?
No one is sure, but hundreds have been found since the 1960s, when scientists first spotted the Little Green Man. Special telescopes called radio telescopes are used to 'listen' for more pulsars.

 Do all pulsars spin at the same speed?
No – even the slowest spin about once every four seconds, but the fastest whizz round many hundreds of times in a single second! Their incredible speeds are thought to be caused by magnetic forces left by a supernova.

What is a black hole?

A black hole is a place in space that forms when a really huge star collapses. Everything around a black hole is sucked into it, like water down a plug hole. The force of gravity in a black hole is so strong that nothing can escape from it – not even light.

Black hole

Amazing! No one has ever seen a black hole. Because beams of light cannot escape black holes, astronomers cannot see them – even with the most powerful telescopes.

What is dark matter?

Dark matter is what scientists call all the stuff in the Universe that they know is there but can't find! They think it might be made of ghostly little particles called neutrinos.

Neutrinos

Is it true?
Black holes turn you into spaghetti.

YES. Scientists think that, in the last moments before you disappeared forever into a black hole, the force of gravity would stretch you until it pulled you apart. They call this being 'spaghettified'!

Dark matter

How do we know that dark matter is there?

Scientists can guess how much matter is in the Universe by measuring how galaxies move. This shows them that stars and planets only make up a small part of the Universe. The rest is invisible!

What is a galaxy?

A galaxy is a group of stars, dust and gases that are held together by gravity. Our galaxy is the Milky Way and contains about 100 billion stars, one of which is our Sun.

Is it true?
All galaxies have names.

NO. Each one that we detect is given numbers and letters, but only some, such as our Milky Way, are given a name as well. 'Galaxy' comes from the Ancient Greek word for 'milk'.

On a clear night you can see the Milky Way

How many galaxies are there?

No one knows for sure. There might be hundreds of billions of galaxies – and new ones are forming right now at the edges of the Universe.

Spiral, oval and irregular galaxies

❓ Are there different kinds of galaxies?

Yes – each galaxy is unlike any other. Some are bright and some are dim. There are three basic galaxy shapes, though – spiral, elliptical (oval) and irregular. Of course, irregular just means no particular shape!

 Amazing! There's a galaxy named after a wide-brimmed Mexican hat. 'Sombrero' is the nickname of galaxy M104. Can you guess the galaxy's shape?

Galaxies can form in many weird and wonderful shapes

What shape is our galaxy?

Our galaxy, the Milky Way, is a spiral galaxy. Viewed from above, it looks like a giant Danish pastry with swirls of white icing. From the side, it looks more like two fried eggs stuck back-to-back!

Amazing! Our galaxy has a twin. Andromeda is the biggest galaxy near the Milky Way. It's the same age and a similar shape, but has many more stars.

What's at the middle of the Milky Way?

The centre (the two 'egg yolks') is called the nuclear bulge. There's probably a monster black hole there, more than a million times bigger than our Sun. Scientists call the black hole Sagittarius A*.

A side view of the Milky Way seen from deep space

How big is the Milky Way?

The Milky Way is almost too big to imagine. It would take one of the world's fastest jets, the Blackbird, about 30 billion years to cross the galaxy.

Is it true?
We're near the centre of the Milky Way.

NO. Our Solar System is closer to the edge, on one of the spiralling arms. Our Sun takes 225 million years to go around the centre once!

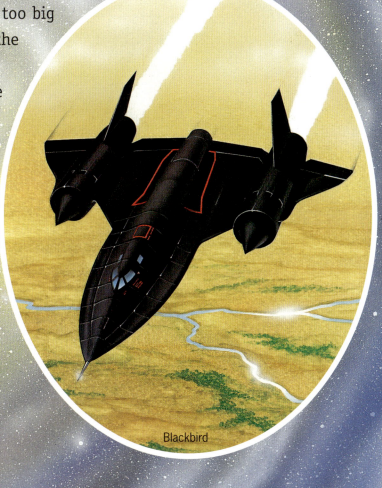

Blackbird

Do galaxies stick together?

Some galaxies are all alone in space, but others huddle together in clusters. Together with 30 other galaxies, our Milky Way and its twin, Andromeda, are part of the Local Group cluster.

Are some galaxies cannibals?

Some scientists think that Andromeda gobbled up other galaxies. It has a double centre, which might be the remains of another galaxy. One day, Andromeda may eat up the Milky Way. It gets 300 km closer to us every second!

Cluster of galaxies

The background shows two galaxies colliding

Amazing! The Local Supercluster contains several thousand galaxies and is more than 100 million light years across. A light year is about 9,461 billion km.

What is a supercluster?

It's a cluster of clouds of clusters! The Local Group that contains our Milky Way is part of a cloud called the Canes Venatici cloud. Together with about six other clouds of galaxies, it is part of the Local Supercluster.

Supercluster of galaxies

 Is it true?
We're part of the biggest galaxy cloud in the Local Supercluster.

NO. The biggest is the Virgo 1 cloud, which contains a fifth of all the galaxies in the supercluster. It's pulling the other clouds in the cluster towards it.

The Moon's gravity pulls a meteorite crashing into its surface

What is gravity?

Gravity is one of the basic forces in the Universe, like electromagnetism. It makes things with mass pull towards each other. More massive objects, such as the Earth, pull smaller objects, such as you, towards them until they stick together.

Isaac Newton

Is it true?
An apple taught us about gravity.

MAYBE. According to legend, super-scientist Isaac Newton first realized how gravity works over 330 years ago after gravity pulled an apple from a tree he was sitting under and it landed on his head!

Is the Universe expanding evenly?

No – the force of gravity stops everything from flying outwards. Lumpy bits of space become even lumpier, moving at different speeds. Gravity locks together little pockets of space and matter, such as galaxies.

Galaxies locked together by the force of gravity

 **Amazing!** There are walls in space! Galaxies aren't evenly spaced through the Universe. They are arranged more like walls around emptier regions of space. One wall has already been measured – it's about a billion light years across!

What is the Great Attractor?

It's a strange little knot in space that has the pulling power of 50 million billion Suns, but is not a black hole.

❓ Is time the same everywhere?

No, time slows down when you're travelling very quickly. Brainy boffin Albert Einstein predicted this odd effect in 1905 but we only proved it a few years ago by sending a super-precise atomic clock into orbit around the Earth.

Albert Einstein

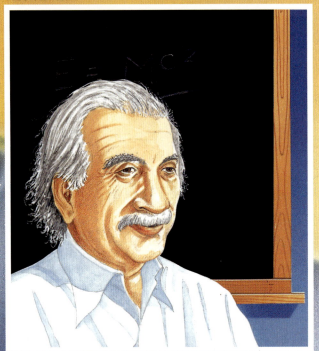

 Is it true?
Einstein was the world's best mathematician.

NO. Although he was very clever, Albert Einstein often asked his wife to check over the trickier sums for him.

Black hole

❓ Could time stand still?

Only if you travelled as fast as the speed of light – which most scientists agree is impossible! Some scientists think that time must stand still inside a black hole, but who'd want to find out?

Amazing! There might be 'tunnels' through space and time, which connect distant parts of the Universe. Scientists call these shortcuts wormholes. If light or even an object entered a wormhole, perhaps it would pass through incredibly quickly. It would be possible to travel billions of kilometres in an instant!

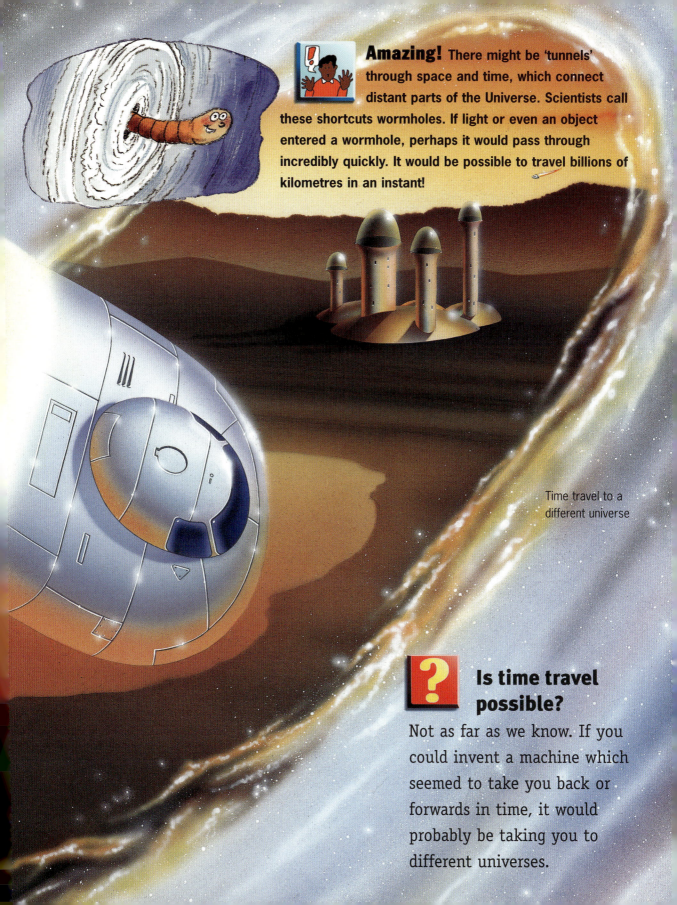

Time travel to a different universe

Is time travel possible?

Not as far as we know. If you could invent a machine which seemed to take you back or forwards in time, it would probably be taking you to different universes.

❓ Is there anybody out there?

We don't know. Life might be such a fluke that it only exists on Earth. But if scientists can find just one other place where there is life, we'll know life's no accident – and that there could be millions of aliens!

❓ How will we find out?

People around the world have joined the Search for Extra-Terrestrial Intelligence (SETI). They spend their spare time on computers, studying waves from space, hoping to find alien messages.

Radio astronomy centre

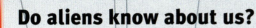 **Do aliens know about us?**
It's unlikely. Humans have only been making radio waves for about a century, so aliens would have to live very nearby to tune in.

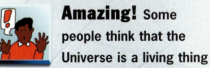 **Amazing!** Some people think that the Universe is a living thing – and that the planets, stars and galaxies are just parts of its 'body'!

Aliens with the Pioneer space probe

 Is it true?
Aliens have visited the Earth.

PROBABLY NOT. There's no proof that aliens have visited us. Even if they could travel at the speed of light, they would take at least four years to reach us from the nearest stars.

101

QUICK QUIZ

1. How long would it take to cross the Universe at the speed of light?

2. Do scientists know what lies beyond the Universe?

3. What name do we give the explosion that started the Universe?

4. How long ago did the Big Bang happen?

5. Is the Universe still expanding?

6. If the Universe were to collapse in on itself, what would the event be called?

7. What is another name for a star nursery?

8. Stars are mostly made of which two gases?

9. Is the Sun a hot, medium-hot or cool star?

10. Is the White Giant Rigel hotter or cooler than our Sun?

11. What are small stars called?

12. What do we call the explosion that happens when a really massive star dies?

13. What is a dead star called?

14. What kind of star is Betelgeuse?

15. What is just 20 km across and weighs 50 times more than the Earth?

16. What kind of star can spin round hundreds of times in one second?

17. Do black holes shine brightly?

18. What do scientists call all the stuff in the Universe that they can't see?

19. Roughly how many stars are there in the Milky Way galaxy?

20. What holds the stars, dust and gases of a galaxy together?

21. What shape is the Milky Way galaxy?

22. Sagittarius A* is the name of the black hole at the centre of which galaxy?

23. What is the name of the Milky Way's twin galaxy?

24. What is 9,461 billion km otherwise known as?

25. Which scientist first realized how gravity works?

Answers on page 138.

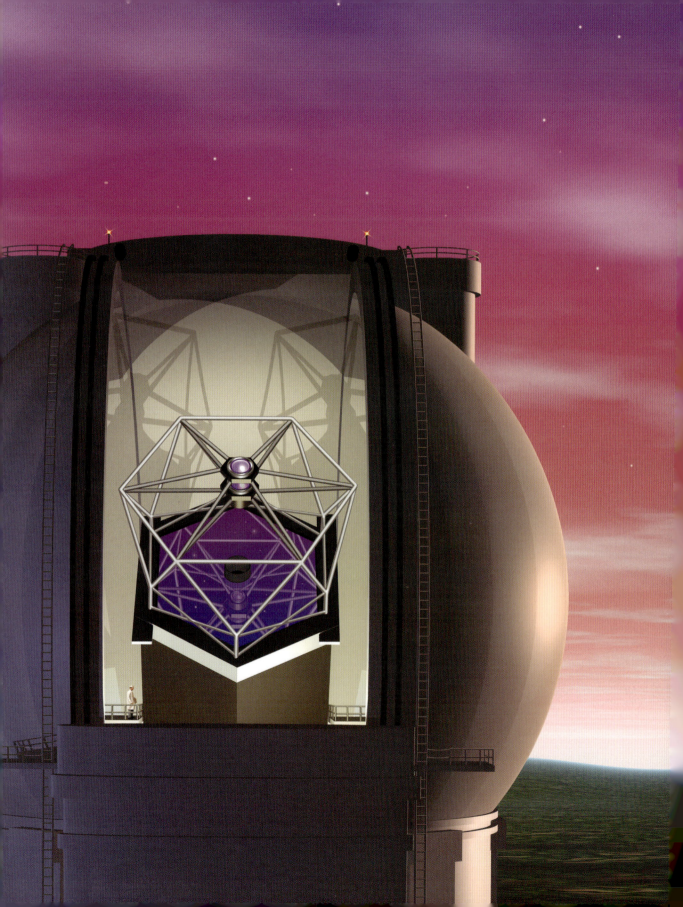

CHAPTER FOUR

LOOKING AT THE NIGHT SKY

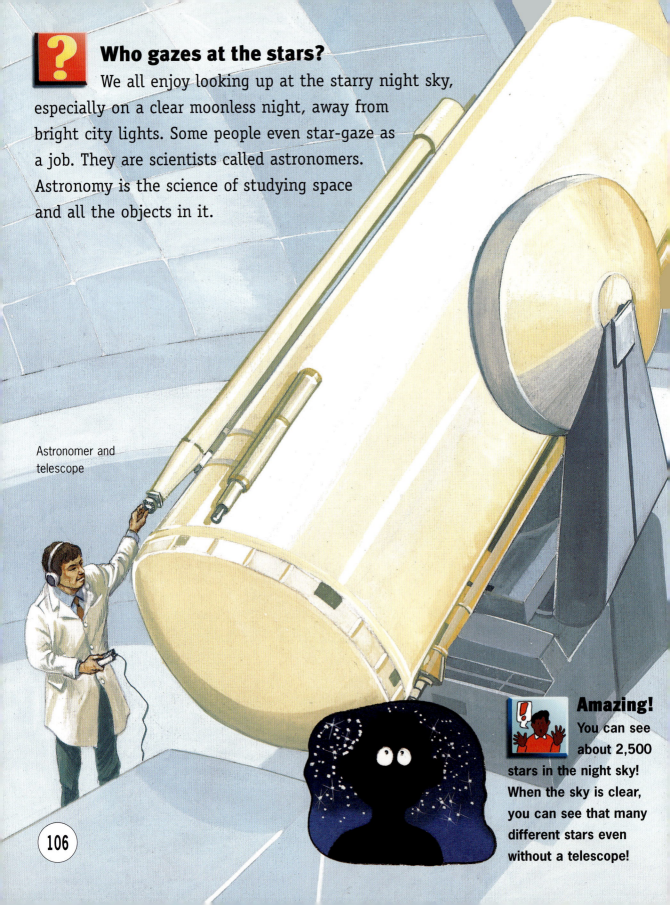

❓ Who gazes at the stars?

We all enjoy looking up at the starry night sky, especially on a clear moonless night, away from bright city lights. Some people even star-gaze as a job. They are scientists called astronomers. Astronomy is the science of studying space and all the objects in it.

Astronomer and telescope

Amazing! You can see about 2,500 stars in the night sky! When the sky is clear, you can see that many different stars even without a telescope!

 ## Can anyone be an astronomer?

Anyone can learn about stars as a hobby, but it takes years of study to do it as a job. You'll need books of star charts and maps, so you can recognise what you see. Binoculars or a telescope will let you see further.

Studying a star chart

 **Is it true?**
You can see the Moon's craters through binoculars.

YES. Binoculars allow you to see the Moon's surface so clearly that you can make out individual craters – from 400,000 km away!

 ## Can you only see the Moon and stars at night?

The Moon and stars are easiest to spot, but even without a telescope you will see meteors (shooting stars) and the brighter planets, such as Venus, Jupiter or Mars. Venus shines white and is nicknamed the 'evening star'. Jupiter looks greeny-blue and Mars glows red.

Meteor shower

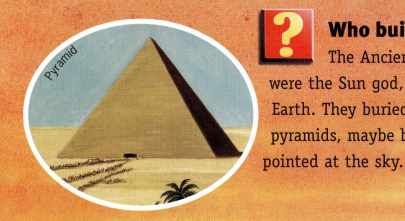

Who built a tomb for the Sun god?
The Ancient Egyptians thought their kings were the Sun god, Ra, who had come down to Earth. They buried kings in huge tombs called pyramids, maybe because the pyramid shape pointed at the sky.

Is it true?
Stonehenge was a primitive computer.

NO. But in the 1960s an American scientist called Gerald Hawkins said it was. He thought Stonehenge was built to work out when eclipses would happen.

Who built a stone circle for the Sun?
No one knows exactly why Stonehenge, a huge stone circle in southwest England, was built by Druids over 4,000 years ago. Its doorway would have framed the sunrise on the longest day of each year.

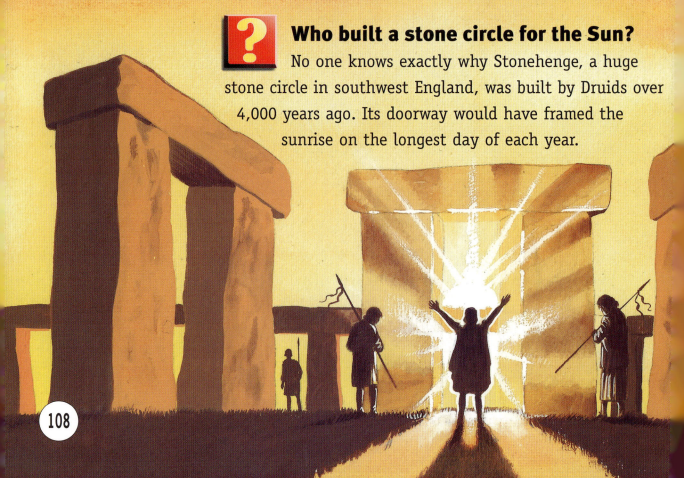

Who thought the sky was a goddess?

The Egyptians thought the night sky was the arched body of a goddess, called Nut. Today we know Nut's body matches the view of the Milky Way from Ancient Egypt.

The Milky Way seen above the pyramids

Ancient Egyptian wall painting showing the goddess Nut

 Amazing! The pyramids have secret Sun passages! Tunnels were built so the buried king could see the sunset on a particular day each spring.

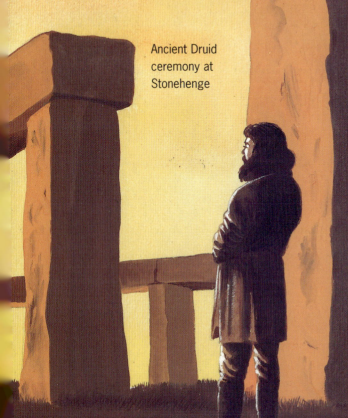
Ancient Druid ceremony at Stonehenge

Who first wrote about the stars?

The Babylonians were the first to write down their findings from studying the stars – around 5,000 years ago! They noticed that stars seem to form patterns, which we call constellations. The Babylonian empire was roughly where Iraq is today.

Babylonian astronomers

Is it true?
The Babylonians were maths wizards.

YES. At first their findings about the night sky were based on looking and guessing. By around 500 BC, the Babylonians used sums to predict exactly when events such as eclipses would happen.

How do we know about the first astronomers?

The Babylonians didn't write on paper like we do. They wrote on clay tablets, so fragments have survived. Scientists called archaeologists dig in the ground for clues about ancient peoples such as the Babylonians.

Amazing! The Babylonians didn't see the same night sky as us. There were no twinkling satellites, and the stars were in different places because our Solar System has moved since then.

Babylonian writing on a clay tablet

What was a Babylonian year like?

The Babylonians worked out a 12-month year. Each month began with the first sight of the crescent Moon. The months were called Nisannu, Ayaru, Simanu, Du'uzu, Abu, Ululu, Tashritu, Arahsamnu, Kislimu, Tebetu, Shabatu and Addaru.

Clay tablet

111

Amazing! An eclipse changed the course of history. Soldiers from Athens in Ancient Greece lost a battle after being spooked by an eclipse of the Moon. Their rivals, the Spartans, were the winners.

❓ Who thought the Sun was as wide as a ruler?

The Greek thinker Heraclitus thought the Sun was just 30 cm across and that a new one was made each morning. So even though the Ancient Greeks were clever, they didn't get everything right!

Heraclitus

Perseus and Andromeda

 ## Who named groups of stars?
In AD 150, the Greek astronomer Ptolemy wrote a book about the stars, describing 48 different constellations (star groups). He named the groups after characters from Greek myths, such as Perseus, the hero who rescued the princess Andromeda. We still use Ptolemy's names today.

Aristotle

Is it true?
People once thought the Earth was flat.

YES. Even up to the 1500s most people believed this. They thought that if you sailed too far, you could fall off the edge!

 ## Who worked out the Earth is round?
The Ancient Greek thinker Aristotle realized that the Earth must be round in the 330s BC. He worked this out when he was watching a lunar eclipse, because he saw that the Earth made a circular shadow on the surface of the Moon.

Why do stars make patterns?

Constellations are the patterns that bright stars seem to make in the night sky, such as a cross, a letter 'W' or the shape of a person. The stars look close together – but that's just how we see them from Earth. Really they are scattered through space and nowhere near each other.

Amazing! The night sky is divided into 88 different star patterns. Nearly 50 were first described 2,000 years ago!

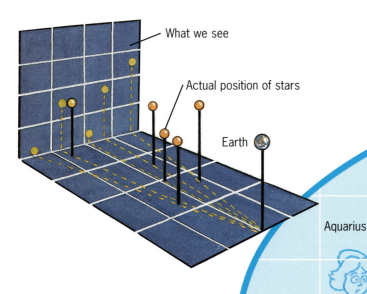

What we see
Actual position of stars
Earth

What is the zodiac?

For astronomers, the zodiac includes the 12 constellations that the Sun passes through during a year. We can't see the Sun doing this, though. The Sun's light is so bright that we cannot see the constellations during the day.

Aquarius
Sagittarius
Virgo
Libra
Capricornus
Scorpius

Zodiac constellations

Which stars make a hunter?

Orion is a constellation named after the legendary Greek hunter. Lots of stars make up the shape. Rigel is the brightest and makes one of the hunter's legs. The next-brightest is Betelgeuse, which shines a reddish colour.

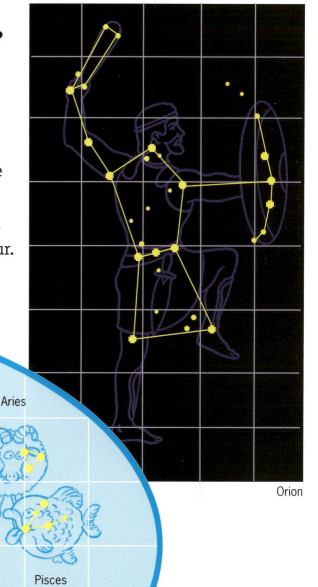

Orion

Leo

Gemini

Aries

Cancer

Pisces

Taurus

Is it true?
Astrologers are specialist astronomers.

NO. The zodiac signs that astrologers use for horoscopes have the same names as the zodiac bands in astronomy. They don't match with the astronomical constellations, though.

How did sailors know where they were going?

Out at sea, there are no landmarks. In the Middle Ages, sailors had special instruments that used the position of the Sun and stars to tell them where they were. These included compasses, astrolabes and cross-staffs.

Sailor and cross-staff

Amazing! The first astrolabes were made 1,500 years ago! Indian and Arab astronomers used pocket-sized instruments called astrolabes in the AD 500s.

Is it true?
Astrolabes only worked at night.

NO. You could use the position of the Sun instead of the stars when you were sailing during the day. You looked at its position compared to the horizon.

How did an astrolabe work?
An astrolabe had two discs, one with a star map, and the other with measuring lines and a pointer. You compared them with the Sun or a star and the horizon to work out your position.

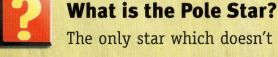
What is the Pole Star?
The only star which doesn't appear to move is above the North Pole. Sailors could tell where they were by looking at the Pole Star – it's lowest in the sky at the Equator.

Path of the stars with the Pole Star in the middle

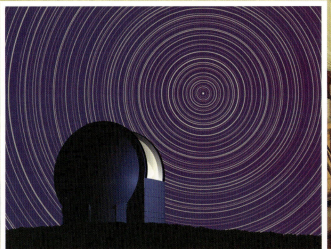

Astrolabe

117

Who made the first telescope?

Hans Lippershey, a Dutch man who made spectacles, probably made the first telescope in 1608. He noticed that if he put two lenses at different ends of a tube and looked through them, objects seemed to be nearer and clearer.

 ## Is it true?
Newton saw a rainbow in his telescope.

YES. Isaac Newton noticed that the edges of objects seemed coloured when you looked through a telescope. That's how he began to work out that clear white light is made up of many different colours.

Hans Lippershey with his telescope

Simple cutaway of a telescope

Newton's reflecting telescope

? How does a telescope work?

The lens (curved piece of glass) at the front end of a telescope gathers light to make an image of an object that is far away. The lens at the back magnifies the image so it can be seen more clearly.

? Who put mirrors in a telescope?

Isaac Newton was the first person to make a mirror or reflecting telescope. He replaced the front lens with a dish-shaped mirror at the back. The mirror reflected the image on to a smaller mirror and then into the eye.

Amazing! Telescopes magnify images (make them bigger) so much that you can even make out Saturn's faint rings – which are about 1.3 billion km away!

Nicolaus Copernicus

 Who said that planets go round the Sun?

Nicolaus Copernicus explained this idea in a book in 1543. The problem was, the Church stated that God had put the Earth at the centre of the Universe. You could be put to death for saying that the Earth went round the Sun.

 Who was put on trial for star-gazing?

Few scientists were brave enough to say that they agreed with Copernicus' findings that the Earth went round the Sun. The Italian astronomer Galileo was – and was put on trial for his ideas in 1634.

 Is it true?
The Church accepted that Galileo was right in the end.

YES. The Church eventually agreed that the Earth and other planets travelled round the Sun. But they didn't do this until 1992 – 350 years after Galileo's death!

Galileo on trial

Who first used a telescope for astronomy?

Galileo started making telescopes in 1609, not long after Lippershey made his. Galileo was the first person to realize how useful a telescope would be for looking at the night sky. Because he could see more clearly, he made lots of important new finds, such as discovering four of Jupiter's moons.

 Amazing! Copernicus explained the seasons. By showing that the Earth goes round the Sun and also spins at the same time, Copernicus explained why some times of the year are warmer than others.

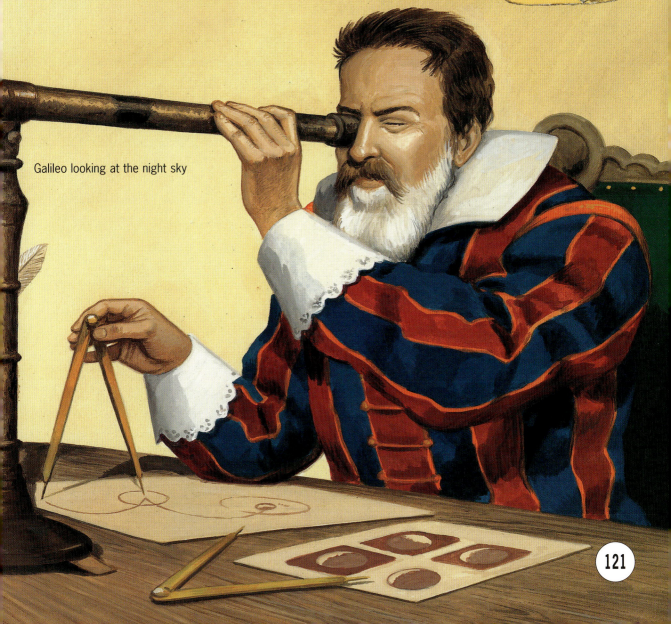
Galileo looking at the night sky

Where do astronomers put their telescopes?

Observatories are buildings where astronomers go to look at the sky. They house the most powerful telescopes on Earth. The telescopes are usually kept in a room with a dome-shaped roof. Observatories have other instruments too, such as very precise clocks, to help keep accurate time and records.

Pulkovo Observatory, Russia

Mount Cerro Observatory, Chile

Where's the best place to build an observatory?

Where you'll get the clearest view! Most are built away from city lights. Mountain-tops are best of all, because they poke above any clouds that might spoil the view.

Is it true?
The Greenwich Observatory houses the most telescopes.

NO. The Kitt Peak National Observatory in Arizona, USA has the most optical telescopes. One of them, the Mayall Telescope, is 4 m across!

Amazing! The Ancient Babylonians used observatories. They did their star-gazing from stepped towers called ziggurats.

Telescope in a domed observatory

How can a telescope see through the roof?

It doesn't have to – an observatory's domed roof is specially designed to slide open at night, so that the picture through the telescope isn't distorted (blurred) by looking through a window. The telescope can be pointed at any place in the sky.

How deep is space?

Early astronomers thought that all the stars were the same distance from us, forming a simple shell around the Earth. Now we know that some stars are relatively close to us, and others are trillions of kilometres away.

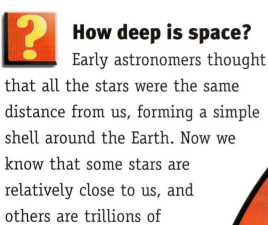

Gaseous clouds in deep space

Amazing!

Galaxies move so quickly they are different colours. The light waves from them change, just as a fire engine's siren sounds lower after it zooms past. We use the colour to measure the galaxies' speed.

Are there candles in space?

Not really. But we can see how far away a galaxy is by the brightness of a special type of star, called a 'standard candle'. The further away the galaxy, the dimmer the candle.

How do you measure the distance to a star?

Watch the tip of your finger as you move it towards your nose. The closer it gets, the more cross-eyed you become! Astronomers can tell the distance to a star by measuring how 'cross-eyed' a pair of telescopes has to be to see it.

NEAREST STAR
40 000 000 000 km

Is it true?
We measure how far the stars are in kilometres.

NO. They're so far away, that we use light years instead. A light year is how far light travels in one year – 9,461 billion km!

Who made the first radio telescope?

Radio telescopes are like giant satellite dishes that pick up invisible radio waves and similar waves, instead of light rays. Unlike light, radio waves can travel through cloud, so radio telescopes can be built just about anywhere! An American called Grote Reber made the first one in the 1930s.

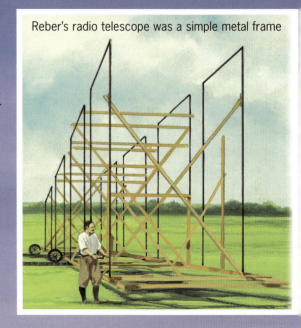
Reber's radio telescope was a simple metal frame

Amazing! A telescope can be 8,000 km long. The Very Long Baseline Array (VLBA) stretches across the USA. It has ten different dishes and produces the best-quality radio images of space from Earth yet!

Which are the most powerful radio telescopes?

The ones that are made up of several different radio dishes, such as the Very Large Array (VLA) in New Mexico, USA. The VLA has 27 dishes, each 25 metres across. Scientists compare the findings from all 27 dishes to get super-accurate results.

VLA, Socorro, New Mexico

Where is the biggest radio telescope?

The world's biggest single-dish radio telescope was built in Puerto Rico in the Caribbean in the 1960s. It is 300 metres across – so it would take you more than ten minutes to walk around the edge of it.

 ### Is it true?
Only ten astronomers are allowed to use the VLA.

NO. It is used by over 500 astronomers a year. Some study our near-neighbours in the Solar System, while others peer way beyond our galaxy to others in deepest space.

Radio telescope, Puerto Rico

Gravity telescope

? What's a gravity telescope?

A gravity telescope uses laser beams to measure its own length. As a gravity wave passes through Earth from space, it stretches the telescope by less than the width of an atom! Four huge gravity telescopes were built at the end of the 1990s.

? Can we see black holes?

We can through a gravity telescope. Although light can't escape a black hole, gravity can. When a black hole swallows up a star, for example, there's a 'ripple' of gravity through space. Gravity wave telescopes spot the ripples.

Black hole

 Amazing! The biggest gravity wave telescope is 4 km long! No one knows yet what new things gravity wave telescopes will help astronomers discover.

What's the weirdest telescope?

The Super Kamiokande telescope near Tokyo is just a big tank full of very pure water, buried deep underground. Very sensitive cameras detect teeny-weeny particles called neutrinos zooming through the Earth, by recording microscopic flashes of light in the water.

Neutrino detector

Is it true?
Neutrinos have a dark secret.

YES. Scientists think the Universe is full of something heavy, which they call dark matter. Neutrinos may be part of it!

Are there telescopes in space?

Yes – the first one went up in the 1960s. Space is a perfect place for looking at the stars. The sky is always dark and cloudless. Away from Earth's pollution and wobbly atmosphere, the stars shine steadily and brightly, instead of twinkling as they do to us on Earth.

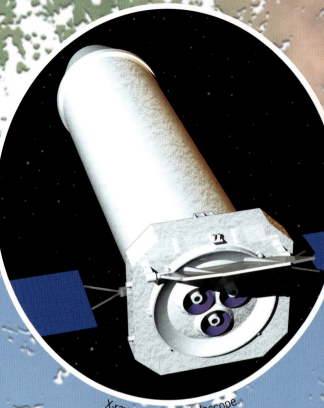
X-ray multi-mirror telescope

Are there observatories in space?

Yes – some observatories use powerful gamma rays, which can penetrate all the gas and dust in the galaxy, to show us what is happening in its centre. The Compton gamma ray observatory was launched into space by the shuttle.

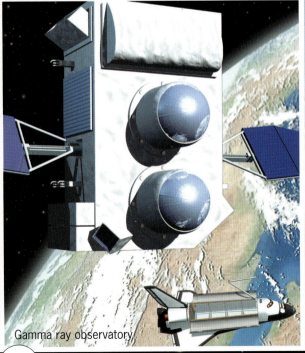
Gamma ray observatory

? Which telescope is in orbit?

The most famous is the Hubble Space Telescope, which was carried into orbit on the space shuttle Discovery in 1990. It circles the Earth every 90 minutes, about 600 km above us. It beams radio signals of information to astronomers on Earth.

Hubble Space Telescope

Amazing!
Hubble runs on Sun-power. Hubble's two 'paddles' are solar panels. They gather energy from the Sun and change it into electrical energy. The energy is used to focus the telescope and beam data home.

Is it true?
Telescopes can look back in time.

YES. Because of the time it takes X-rays to travel through space, Chandra can see quasars as they were ten billion years ago!

❓ What's better than a powerful telescope?

Seeing for yourself in close-up – but it's too dangerous and expensive to send astronomers deep into space. That's why space probes are such important tools. Space probes are fitted with cameras. They beam back close-up photos of faraway planets and comets.

Cassini-Huygens spacecraft

Amazing! Chandra is a billion times more powerful than the first X-ray telescope. If telescopes keep improving at this rate, we'll be able to see the farthest edges of the Universe in 30 years' time!

Is it true?
A probe found a watery world.

YES. The Voyager 2 probe photographed what might be water on Jupiter's moon, Europa. If there is life out there, probes will probably find it first.

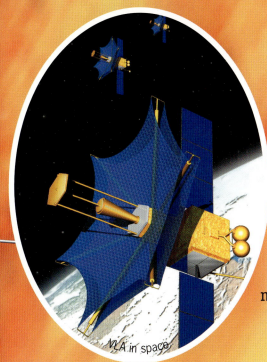
VLA in space

? Could we build Very Large Arrays in space?

Scientists are already testing a cluster of satellites that fly in perfect formation, using laser beams. The same technology will be used to create a string of small satellite telescopes, making one huge 'eye' in space.

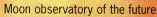
Moon observatory of the future

 ### Could we build an observatory on the Moon?

The dark side of the Moon would be a perfect site. Always pointing away from the Earth, it is shielded from man-made X-rays. But building there would be very expensive.

QUICK QUIZ

1. What name is given to the science of studying space and all the objects in it?
2. Roughly how many stars can you see in the night sky?
3. What is the name of the huge stone circle built in southwest England over 4,000 years ago?
4. What are star groups (or patterns) called?
5. Which Ancient Greek named 48 constellations?

6. What was the Ancient Greek thinker Aristotle watching when he worked out that the Earth must be round?
7. How many constellations are there?
8. One of the constellations is named after a legendary Greek hunter – what is it called?
9. What name do we call the group of 12 constellations that the Sun passes through each year?
10. Which star is the only star that doesn't appear to move?

11. When were the first astrolabes made?
12. Can a telescope make out something that is 1.3 billion km away?
13. In 1543, who said that the planets go round the Sun?
14. How many of Jupiter's moons did Galileo discover by looking through a telescope?
15. What is the name given to the building where a powerful telescope is kept?

16. What were Babylonian stepped towers called?

17. What is the unit of measurement used to measure how far away stars are?

18. In which country will you find the Very Large Array radio telescope?

19. What can you detect in space through a gravity telescope that you can't see with an ordinary telescope?

20. In which country will you find the Super Kamiokande telescope?

21. Seen from space, do the stars appear to twinkle, or do they shine steadily?

22. Which famous space telescope circles the Earth every 90 minutes?

23. Do space probes take close-up or long-distance photos?

24. Where might you find a watery world?

25. Which side of the Moon would be the best side to put an observatory, the dark side or the side we see from Earth?

Answers on page 139.

QUICK QUIZ ANSWERS CHAPTER ONE

1. 'Solar' means 'of the Sun'.
2. Eight planets orbit the Sun.
3. Mars has two moons.
4. Sunspots are slightly cooler than the rest of the Sun.
5. Venus is the hottest planet.

6. Yes, travelling at 173,000 kph, Mercury moves faster than a space rocket.
7. The planet Venus is sometimes called the 'evening star'.
8. Venus is named after the Roman goddess of love and beauty.
9. About three-quarters of the Earth's surface is covered in water.
10. Molten iron forms the Earth's core.

11. The first astronauts to visit the Moon landed on the Sea of Tranquillity.
12. Space rocks or meteorites that strike the Moon's surface make the craters.
13. The biggest volcano in the Solar System is called Olympus Mons.
14. Jupiter's Great Red Spot is a giant storm.
15. Io smells of rotten eggs!

16. Jupiter has 50 moons in all.
17. Saturn is much, much bigger than Earth (about 740 times bigger!).
18. Titan is Saturn's biggest moon.
19. Summer lasts for 42 years on Uranus.
20. Uranus is bluish-green.

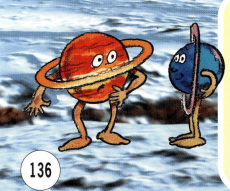

21. Triton is covered in ice.
22. Mercury is the smallest planet in the Solar System.
23. Russia is actually bigger than Pluto!
24. A comet is made of rock and ice.
25. A meteor is another name for a shooting star.

QUICK QUIZ ANSWERS CHAPTER TWO

1. The Chinese made the first rockets.

2. A V2 was a rocket missile used by the Germans in World War II.

3. A rocket has to reach 40,000 kph to escape from Earth's gravity.

4. Laika was famous for being the first living creature in space.

5. Russian pilot Yuri Gagarin was the first person in space.

6. Astronauts and cosmonauts return to Earth in a capsule.

7. A heat shield protects a capsule from burning up on re-entry to Earth's atmosphere.

8. American Neil Armstrong was first to set foot on the Moon.

9. Apollo 13's oxygen tanks exploded.

10. Apollo 15 carried a Lunar Rover to the Moon.

11. The first space shuttle was called Columbia.

12. Yes, the Russian space shuttle was called Buran, but it only flew once.

13. An astronaut's space suit is kept cool by a water-cooling system.

14. The first cosmonauts wore just their underwear for take-off!

15. Astronauts drink from cups with lids and use straws.

16. On Skylab, the shower water was sucked away by a vacuum cleaner!

17. Spiders were sent into space to see if it affected how they spun their webs.

18. ISS stands for International Space Station.

19. MMU stands for Manned Manoeuvring Unit.

20. The space shuttle's arm was used for picking up things in space.

21. Vikings 1 and 2 collected samples and took photos.

22. The radio-controlled car that studied soil and rock samples on Mars was called Sojourner.

23. Sputnik 1 was the first satellite in space.

24. Satellites are powered by energy from the Sun.

25. Halley's Comet was photographed by the Giotto space probe.

QUICK QUIZ ANSWERS CHAPTER THREE

1. It would take at least 15 billion years to cross the Universe at the speed of light.

2. No, scientists don't know what lies beyond the Universe.

3. The explosion that started the Universe is called the Big Bang.

4. Scientists argue that the Big Bang happened between 12 and 15 billion years ago.

5. Yes, the Universe is still expanding.

6. If the Universe were to collapse in on itself, the event would be called the Big Crunch.

7. A star nursery is also called a nebula.

8. Stars are mostly made of hydrogen and helium.

9. The Sun is a medium-hot star.

10. The White Giant Rigel is much hotter than our Sun.

11. Small stars are called dwarfs.

12. When a really massive star dies, the explosion is called a supernova.

13. A dead star is called a black dwarf.

14. Betelgeuse is a red giant.

15. A neutron star can be just 20 km across and weigh 50 times more than the Earth.

16. Pulsars can spin round hundreds of times in one second.

17. No, not even light can escape from a black hole.

18. Dark matter is what scientists call all the stuff in the Universe that they can't see.

19. There are about 100 billion stars in the Milky Way galaxy.

20. Gravity holds the stars, dust and gases of a galaxy together.

21. The Milky Way galaxy is spiral-shaped.

22. Sagittarius A* is the name of the black hole at the centre of the Milky Way galaxy.

23. The Milky Way's twin galaxy is the Andromeda galaxy.

24. 9,461 billion km is also known as a light year.

25. Isaac Newton was the scientist who first realized how gravity works.

QUICK QUIZ ANSWERS CHAPTER FOUR

1. Astronomy is the name given to the science of studying space and all the objects in it.

2. You can see about 2,500 stars in the night sky.

3. Stonehenge is the name of the huge stone circle built in southwest England over 4,000 years ago.

4. Star groups (or patterns) are called constellations.

5. Ptolemy was the Ancient Greek who named 48 constellations.

6. Aristotle was watching a lunar eclipse when he worked out that the Earth must be round.

7. There are 88 different constellations.

8. Orion is the constellation named after a legendary Greek hunter.

9. The zodiac is the name given to the group of 12 constellations that the Sun passes through each year.

10. The Pole Star is the only star that doesn't appear to move.

11. The first astrolabes were made 1,500 years ago.

12. Yes, you can see the faint rings around Saturn, which is 1.3 billion km away.

13. Nicolaus Copernicus said, in 1543, that the planets go around the Sun.

14. Galileo discovered four of Jupiter's moons through a telescope.

15. An observatory is the name given to the building where a powerful telescope is kept.

16. Babylonian stepped towers were called 'ziggurats'.

17. A light year is the unit of measurement used to measure how far away the stars are.

18. The Very Large Array radio telescope is in the United States.

19. A gravity telescope can detect black holes, which can't be seen through an ordinary telescope.

20. You will find the Super Kamiokande telescope in Japan.

21. Seen from space, the stars shine steadily.

22. The Hubble Space Telescope circles the Earth every 90 minutes.

23. Space probes take close-up photos of faraway planets and comets.

24. There might be water on Jupiter's moon, Europa.

25. The best side of the Moon to put an observatory would be the dark side.

Glossary

Asteroid A small rocky body which orbits the Sun.

Astrology Using patterns in the sky as a guide to daily life.

Astronaut Someone who travels into space. The word means 'sailor of the stars'.

Astronomy The science of space-watching.

Atmosphere The gases or air surrounding a planet.

Axis The imaginary line around which a planet spins.

Big Bang The huge explosion that created the Universe around 15 billion years ago.

Black hole A place in space with such strong gravity that not even light can escape from it.

Capsule A small spacecraft with room for one or two crew.

Comet A body of ice and rock with a long glowing tail that orbits the Sun.

Constellation The pattern that stars seem to make in the sky, from our viewpoint on Earth.

Core The middle of something.

Cosmology The science of how the Universe (or 'cosmos') works.

Cosmonaut A Russian or Soviet astronaut. The word means 'sailor of the Universe'.

Data Information.

Eclipse When light from the Sun or Moon is blocked out. A solar eclipse is when the Moon passes between the Earth and Sun, casting a shadow on the Earth. A lunar eclipse is when Earth passes between the Moon and Sun.

Galaxy A family of star systems that are held together by gravity. Our Solar System is in the Milky Way galaxy.

Lens A curved piece of glass.

Meteorite A space rock that hits the Earth.

Meteoroid A small lump of space rock.

Module A section of a space station.

Moon An object in space orbiting a planet.

Nebula A huge cloud of gas and dust where new stars are born.

Observatory A place that houses telescopes and other instruments for viewing the sky.

Orbit To travel around.

Payload The cargo that a rocket carries into space.

Planet A body of gas or rock orbiting a star. Planets are not massive enough to be stars. They shine because they reflect the light of the star they are orbiting.

Poles The points at either end of a planet's axis, known as the north and south poles.

Pulsar A small, dense, fast-spinning neutron star that gives out regular pulses of light and radio waves.

Quasar A region of space giving off more energy than almost any other.

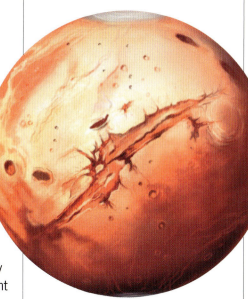

Seasons Different times of the year, when Earth's weather and life change according to the position of the Sun in the sky.

Solar panels Mirrors that capture energy from the Sun and turn it into electricity.

Solar power Power made from the Sun.

Solar System Our Sun and everything that travels around it.

Stage A section of a rocket. Rockets usually have three stages.

Star A huge ball of super-hot burning gas.

Telescope An instrument that makes distant objects seem bigger and nearer. They collect light, radio waves, X-rays or other waves.

Ultraviolet rays Harmful rays from the Sun.

Universe Everything that exists.

Vacuum An empty space with no air.

Wormhole A short cut between two different parts of space.

Index

A
Aldrin, Buzz 50
alien life 23, 27, 66, 86, 100–101, 133
Andromeda 92, 94
animals in space 46, 47, 58
Apollo missions 48, 50, 51
Ariane rocket 44
Ariel 30
Aristotle 113
Armstrong, Neil 50
asteroids 10, 23, 36
astrolabes 116, 117
astrologers 115
astronomy 106, 110–111, 114, 116, 124, 127

B
Babylonians 110–111, 123
Betelgeuse 85, 115
Big Bang 76–77
Big Crunch 78, 79
binary stars 82
binoculars 20, 107
black dwarfs 85
black holes 88, 89, 92, 98, 128
bones, weakening 59
Braun, Wernher von 43
Buran 53

C
Callisto 26, 27
Canes Venatici cloud 95
carbon 81
carbon dioxide 22
Cassini space probe 67
Challenger 53
Chandra 131, 132
Charon 34
chimpanzees 47
Christy, Jim 34
Collins, Michael 50
Columbia 52, 53

comets 10, 36, 66
communication 61
constellations 113, 114–115
Copernicus, Nicolaus 120, 121
Cordelia 30
cosmologists 78, 79
craters 14, 20, 21, 27, 107

D
dark matter 89, 129
day and night 19
days and years 17, 111
Deimos 23
Discovery 131
dwarfs 83, 84, 85

E
Earth 10, 11, 13, 18–19, 75, 120
  flat Earth theory 113
  gravity 44, 65, 96
  life on Earth 18
  magnetism 19
  seasons 121
  size 16
eating and drinking 56, 57
eclipses 13, 108, 110, 112, 113
Einstein, Albert 98
Europa 27, 133

F
fossils 23

G
Gagarin, Yuri 46
galaxies 75, 90–95, 97, 124
Galileo 27, 120, 121
gamma ray observatory 130
Ganymede 26, 27
gas giants 24
gases 24, 31, 33, 80, 81
Giotto space probe 66
Goddard, Robert 43
gravity 10, 21, 23, 44, 65, 69, 79, 88, 89, 96–97, 128
gravity telescopes 128

gravity waves 128
Great Attractor 97
Great Red Spot 25
gunpowder 42

H
Halley's Comet 36, 66
helium 24, 31, 81
Heraclitus 112
Herschel, William 30, 31
holidays in space 69
Horsehead Nebula 80
Hubble Space Telescope 60, 131
Huygens space probe 67
hydrogen 24, 31, 81

I
ice 22, 27, 28, 34, 36
International Space Station (ISS) 59, 60
Io 26, 27
iron 19, 22
Irwin, James 51

J
jet engines 42
Jupiter 10, 11, 24–25, 26, 27, 107, 121

K
Kitt Peak National Observatory 123

L
Laika 46
Large Magellanic Cloud 84
Leonov, Alexei 47, 49
light years 125
Lippershey, Hans 118
Little Green Man (LGM) 86, 87
Local Supercluster 94, 95
Lowell, Percival 34
Lunar Rover 51

M
Magellan space probe 67
magnetism 19
Manned Manoeuvring Unit (MMU) 60

Mars 10, 11, 22–23, 62–63, 68, 107
Mars Pathfinder 62–63
Mercury 10, 11, 14–15
meteor showers 37, 107
meteoroids 37
meteors 37, 107
methane 31
Milky Way 90, 92–93, 94, 109
Mir space station 56
Miranda 30
Mission Control 49
Moon 11, 13, 20–21, 107, 133
    Moon Bases 68, 69
    Moon landings 50–51
moons 11, 23, 26–27, 29, 30, 33, 34

N
nebulae 80, 81
Neptune 11, 32–33, 35
neutrinos 89, 129
neutron stars 86
Newton, Isaac 96, 118, 119
nitrogen 33
nuclear reaction 81
Nut (Egyptian goddess) 109

O
Oberon 30
observatories 122–123, 130, 133
Ophelia 30
orbits 10, 15, 19, 21, 35, 44, 58, 120
Orion 115
oxygen 18, 68

P
payloads 44
Phobos 23
Pioneer 10 space probe 66
planets 10–35, 36
Pluto 14, 34–35
Pole Star 117
poles 19, 22, 30, 33
Ptolemy 113
pulsars 86–87
pyramids 108, 109

Q
quasars 131

R
Ra (Egyptian Sun god) 108
radio telescopes 87, 126–127
radio waves 101, 126
red giants 85
returning to Earth 48–49, 53
Ride, Sally 47
Rigel 83, 115
rings 11, 28, 29, 119
robots 61, 63
rockets 42–45, 52, 62, 65

S
Salyut 1 58
satellites 44, 64–65, 133
Saturn 10, 11, 28-29, 67, 119
Saturn 5 rocket 45
Scott, David 51
Search for Extra-Terrestrial Intelligence (SETI) 100
seasons 121
shooting stars 37, 107
silicon 81
Sirius B 84
Skylab space station 57
Sojourner 63
solar power 65, 131
Solar System 10–37, 75, 93, 111
Sombrero 91
space capsules 46, 48-49
space hotels 69
space pirates 68
space probes 44, 62–63, 66–67, 132–133
space rock 10, 14, 36
space shuttles 52–53, 56, 57, 61
space sickness 57
space stations 56, 57, 58–59
space suits 54–55
space tankers 69
spacewalks 47, 54, 55
spiders 58
Sputnik 1 64
Sputnik 2 46
star nurseries 80
stars 75, 80–87, 88, 106, 113, 114–115, 117, 124, 125
Stonehenge 108
storms 25, 32
sulphur 26
Sun 10, 12–13, 82, 85, 93, 112, 114, 120
sunspots 13
Super Kamiokande telescope 129
supercluster 94, 95
supernovas 84, 86, 87

T
telescopes 69, 77, 87, 118–119, 121, 122, 123, 126–131
temperatures 12, 15, 32, 76
Tereshkova, Valentina 47
Thrust SSC 42
time 98
time travel 99
Titan 29
Titania 30
toilet, using the 55
tools 60
Triton 32, 33

U
ultraviolet (UV) rays 12
Umbriel 30
underwater training 61
Universe 74–79, 101
Uranus 11, 30–31, 32

V
V2 rocket 43
Venus 10, 11, 15, 16–17, 107
Very Long Array (VLA) 126, 127
Very Long Baseline Array (VLBA) 126
Viking space probes 62
Virgo 1 cloud 95
volcanoes 23, 26
Voskhod 49
Vostok 46, 48
Voyager 2 67, 133

W
washing 57
water 18, 22, 23, 24, 27, 63, 133
white dwarfs 84
white giants 83
winds 25, 32
women astronauts 47, 55
wormholes 99

Z
ziggurats 123
zodiac 114–115